MW00364936

'Start with the central eve[...]
carefully curated portions o[...]
chunks of biblical-theological wisdom from Chris Wright and what
emerges is the book before you. More than a book, though, this is
an invitation to come on a journey. It's a journey that takes in six
breathtaking vistas – the defeat of evil, the destruction of death, the
forgiveness of sinners, the reconciliation of enemies, the governance
of history, the restoration of creation – all of which converge in the
cross of Christ.

Along the way, the opportunity to reflect on passages across
Scripture as a whole brings with it a joyous reminder that the cross
is not just one moment in the Bible's story, but that which stands as
the climax of the entire history of salvation. So, here's my advice:
take the journey; invite others to join you; be amazed again at what
Christ has done for us and for all creation.'
Antony Billington, Theology Advisor, London Institute for
Contemporary Christianity, and Senior Pastor, Beacon Church,
Ashton-in-Makerfield, near Wigan

'A reminder of what lies at the heart of the Christian faith, distilled
with intelligence and passion. I opened this on a day when I wanted
someone else to do the thinking for me, and I loved it.'
Jeremy Vine, broadcaster

'After skimming this wonderful manuscript over the summer
months, I certainly know what book I want to read slowly and
carefully during Lent next year. In easily accessible daily readings,
comments, dramatic meditations and questions, the deeply personal
and yet comprehensive and global significance of Easter is unpacked
by careful exposition of biblical texts over the weeks of Lent. This
will, without doubt, greatly deepen your understanding of the cross
and resurrection and, quite possibly, change your life! I strongly
recommend it.'
Richard Winter, MB, BS, past member of the Royal College of
Psychiatrists, Emeritus Professor of Applied Theology and
Counseling, Covenant Theological Seminary, St Louis, Missouri

THE RADICAL RECONCILER

All the royalties from this book have been irrevocably assigned to Langham Literature. Langham Literature is a ministry of Langham Partnership, founded by John Stott. Chris Wright is the International Ministries Director.

Langham Literature provides Majority World preachers, scholars and seminary libraries with evangelical books and electronic resources through publishing and distribution, grants and discounts. They also foster the creation of indigenous evangelical books in many languages through writers' grants, strengthening local evangelical publishing houses and investment in major regional literature projects.

For further information on Langham Literature, and the rest of Langham Partnership, visit the website at <www.langham.org>.

THE RADICAL RECONCILER

Lent in all the Scriptures

Chris Wright
with
John Stott

INTER-VARSITY PRESS
36 Causton Street, London SW1P 4ST, England
Email: ivp@ivpbooks.com
Website: www.ivpbooks.com

First published 2019

British Library Cataloguing-in-Publication Data

A catalogue record for this book is available from the British Library.

ISBN: 978–1–78359–944–8
eBook ISBN: 978–1–78359–945–5

Set in 11/14 pt Minion Pro
Typeset in Great Britain by CRB Associates, Potterhanworth, Lincolnshire
Printed in Great Britain by Ashford Colour Press Ltd, Gosport, Hampshire

*Inter-Varsity Press publishes Christian books that are true to the Bible and that
communicate the gospel, develop discipleship and strengthen the church for its mission
in the world.*

*IVP originated within the Inter-Varsity Fellowship, now the Universities and Colleges
Christian Fellowship, a student movement connecting Christian Unions in universities
and colleges throughout Great Britain, and a member movement of the International
Fellowship of Evangelical Students. Website: www.uccf.org.uk. That historic association
is maintained, and all senior IVP staff and committee members subscribe to the
UCCF Basis of Faith.*

Contents

Contents

Week 3
SINNERS FORGIVEN

Week 4
ENEMIES RECONCILED

Contents

Week 5
HISTORY GOVERNED

Holy Week
CREATION RESTORED

Contents

EASTER DAY

INTRODUCTION

'It is finished!'

These were almost the very last words that Jesus spoke from the cross (see John 19:30). Actually, it was probably more like a shout – or the closest he could get to a shout as he approached an agonizing death.

But what did Jesus mean? He meant much more than merely, 'It's over at last.' This was a cry of achievement, of mission accomplished. Jesus was not just stating the obvious – his life was coming to an end. There could be no other outcome once you were nailed to a cross, though it could take days for that gruesome ending to come. No, Jesus was affirming that something had now been conclusively completed. This was a moment in history. He had accomplished what he had come to earth to do.

Now it has to be said that people don't normally talk about their impending death as their greatest achievement in life. Yet that is exactly what Jesus is doing. After those six hours of agony on the cross, whose physical and spiritual depth we cannot begin to fathom, Jesus knows that his task is complete. The victory is won. God the Son has accomplished once and for all in history what God the Father, Son and Holy Spirit had planned for all eternity.

And what exactly had the cross of Christ accomplished? What was 'finished' as Jesus died?

The answer will immediately rise to your lips, if you are a Christian believer. Jesus accomplished my salvation. Jesus died *for me*, bearing my sin and its consequences, so that I can be forgiven, be reconciled to God and receive eternal life, a share in the kingdom of God and the assured prospect of resurrection bodily life with him in the new creation.

Wonderful, heart-warming, life-transforming gospel truths! We look forward to celebrating them again at the end of Lent, when we arrive once again at Easter. And the glorious *personal assurance* that flows from the cross of Christ resonates through the centuries, of course, in the reinforcing lyrics of countless hymns and spiritual songs that we will sing.

But, having articulated that liberating personal truth with gratitude and rejoicing, we have not said all there is to be said about what Christ accomplished. Not even the half has been told – far, far from it. When we explore the meaning of the cross in the light of the whole Bible, and especially through the ways the New Testament writers speak of it, we stand absolutely amazed at the cosmic scale and scope of what Christ accomplished there.

In this comprehensive and exciting biblical journey through Lent, we will explore the following six great dimensions.

Through the cross,

- evil powers are defeated and their prisoners liberated, and ultimately all evil will be destroyed, on the basis of what Christ suffered here;
- death is destroyed, and life and immortality are brought to life;
- God bore in his own self the cost and consequence of human sin so that sinners can be forgiven;
- God made peace, and enemies are reconciled;
- history is brought under the governance of the Lamb who was slain;
- the whole of creation has been reconciled to God.

'It is finished!' cried Jesus. And that means *everything*. Every dimension of God's redemptive plan for his whole creation was accomplished at the cross. And then God authoritatively vindicated his Son and proclaimed his victory to all creation by raising Jesus from the dead. Jesus accomplished the radical reconciliation of all things in heaven and on earth, through his blood shed on the cross. He is, as our title says, 'The Radical Reconciler'.

So, as we journey through Lent, we shall prepare for Easter by reflecting on these great dimensions of the accomplishment of the cross. We shall begin each week on the successive Sundays in Lent with a reading from Scripture and an extended quotation from John Stott. Most of these will be taken from his classic book *The Cross of Christ*. If you haven't encountered this book yet, then I hope that this series of meditations will whet your appetite to get hold of it and nourish your own soul with its rich diet of biblical truth. John Stott always said it was the most important book he ever wrote (of more than fifty!), and I think he was right. I read it again myself after many years, in preparation for this book, and it was so, so, refreshing!

And then, in the remaining days of each week, we shall explore one of those six great accomplishments of the cross through a variety of scriptures from both Testaments. I think you'll find that you'll need to keep your Bible open after reading the set Bible passage, as we work through each daily meditation. Lent begins on Ash Wednesday. So, after an initial reflection from John Stott on the meaning of self-denial – a prominent theme in Lent – we shall anticipate Easter with three meditations on the gospel narratives surrounding Christ's death.

Our subtitle is 'Lent in All the Scriptures'. I don't mean by that, of course, that all the texts we survey en route, many of them from the Old Testament, are all 'about the cross' – or even all 'about Jesus'. What I have tried to do in my selection of texts from the Old Testament, the Gospels and the Epistles is to survey the broad contours of some of the major biblical themes that converge at the cross. We need to see the scale of the problem God addresses in the great overarching biblical narrative. And we need to see the scope of God's accomplishment in redeeming fallen humanity and a broken creation.

It is said that the way to a man's heart is through his stomach. Satisfying a physical hunger can move the emotions. I think John Stott might have said that the way to a Christian's heart is through

Introduction

the mind (or, if he didn't, I've coined the phrase posthumously for him! He did write a book entitled *Your Mind Matters*; IVP, 2007). My point is that satisfying our spiritual hunger with biblical nourishment should feed and enrich our devotions. One reason why the Psalms are so rich and powerful is that they feed the mind with God's truth, and at the same time nourish our souls and move our hearts. So it is my hope and prayer that, as we chew over many passages of God's Word together, you will find these daily reflections as nourishing to savour as I have found them to write.

A final word about style. In order to engage with familiar stories, I will occasionally 'get under the skin' of the character, to bring the narrative alive and highlight key themes. I trust that this appeal to your imagination will contribute to the central aim: that of bringing home to our hearts and minds the wonder of the gospel of Christ.

Ash Wednesday
Self-denial

Rend your heart
   and not your garments.
Return to the LORD your God,
   for he is gracious and compassionate,
slow to anger and abounding in love,
   and he relents from sending calamity.
(Joel 2:13)

Whoever wants to be my disciple must deny themselves and
take up their cross and follow me.
(Mark 8:34)

To deny ourselves is to behave towards ourselves as Peter did
towards Jesus when he denied him three times. The verb is the same
(*aparneomai*). He disowned him, repudiated him, turned his back
on him.

Self-denial is not denying to ourselves luxuries such as chocolates,
cakes, cigarettes and cocktails (though it may include this); it is
actually denying or disowning ourselves, renouncing our supposed
right to go our own way. To deny oneself is to turn away from
the idolatry of self-centredness. Paul must have been referring to the
same thing when he wrote that those who belong to Christ 'have
crucified the sinful nature with its passions and desires' (Gal. 5:24).
No picture could be more graphic than that: an actual taking of the
hammer and nails to fasten our slippery fallen nature to the cross
and thus do it to death. The traditional word for this is 'mortifica-
tion'; it is the sustained determination by the power of the Holy
Spirit to 'put to death the misdeeds of the body', so that through
this death we may live in fellowship with God . . .

Our 'self' is a complex entity of good and evil, glory and shame, which on that account requires that we develop even more subtle attitudes to ourselves.

What we are (our self or personal identity) is partly the result of the creation (the image of God), and partly the result of the Fall (the image defaced). The self we are to deny, disown and crucify is our fallen self, everything within us that is incompatible with Jesus Christ (hence his commands 'let him deny *himself*' and then 'let him follow *me*'). The self we are to affirm and value is our created self, everything within us that is compatible with Jesus Christ (hence his statement that if we lose ourselves by self-denial, we shall find ourselves). True self-denial (the denial of our false, fallen self) is not the road to self-destruction, but the road to self-discovery.

So then, whatever we are by creation we must affirm: our rationality, our sense of moral obligation, our sexuality (whether masculinity or femininity), our family life, our gifts of aesthetic appreciation and artistic creativity, our stewardship of the fruitful earth, our hunger for love and experience of community, our awareness of the transcendent majesty of God, and our inbuilt urge to fall down and worship him. All this (and more) is part of our created humanness. True, it has been tainted and twisted by sin. Yet Christ came to redeem it, not destroy it. So we must gratefully and positively affirm it.

What we are by the Fall, however, we must deny or repudiate: our irrationality, our moral perversity, our blurring of sexual distinctives and lack of sexual self-control, the selfishness which spoils our family life, our fascination with the ugly, our lazy refusal to develop God's gifts, our pollution and spoliation of the environment, the anti-social tendencies which inhibit true community, our proud autonomy, and our idolatrous refusal to worship the living and true God. All this (and more) is part of our fallen humanness. Christ came not to redeem this, but to destroy it. So we must strenuously deny or repudiate it . . .

We must be true to our true self and false to our false self. We must be fearless in affirming all that we are by creation, redemption and calling, and ruthless in disowning all that we are by the Fall.

Moreover, the cross of Christ teaches us both attitudes. On the one hand, the cross is the God-given measure of the value of our true self, since Christ loved us and died for us. On the other hand, it is the God-given model for the denial of our false self, since we are to nail it to the cross and so put it to death. Or, more simply, standing before the cross, we see simultaneously our worth and our unworthiness, since we perceive the greatness of his love in dying, and the greatness of our sin in causing him to die.

John Stott, *The Cross of Christ*, pp. 323–330

Thursday
Three scriptures in a cup

Bible reading: Matthew 26:17–30

Foreboding and tension

Matthew 26 just keeps getting darker, doesn't it? We read of:

- an anointing for burial (verses 1–13);
- planning for a betrayal (verses 14–16);
- preparation for a memorial (the Passover – verses 17–30);
- prediction of a denial (verses 31–35);
- overwhelming struggle (verses 36–46).

You will know those words that Jesus spoke at the Last Supper, but have you noticed how they are slung between betrayal and denial, between Judas's deceit and Peter's boasting? That is the dark backdrop to our precious sacrament of Holy Communion, when we remember the Lord's death. Those are the sin-laden realities, in which we all share, that made it necessary.

It was a Passover meal, of course. And that's when they would celebrate the exodus with a longing that God would come once more and deliver his people, as of old. There were set words for the host to say during the meal. But at two points, with the breaking of bread and the pouring out of one of the cups of wine, Jesus aston-ished his disciples with different words of his own.

Changing the words

There were four cups of wine at Passover (corresponding to the four promises of God in Exodus 6:6–7), and the third was called the cup of redemption or cup of blessing. It was probably while pouring out this cup that Jesus broke the traditional Passover liturgy with startling new words.

> This is my blood of the covenant,
> which is poured out for many
> for the forgiveness of sins.
> (Matthew 26:28)

How many times have you heard those familiar words? But try to hear them for the first time in that upper room, with the disciples who knew their Scriptures very well. Jesus is pulling together phrases from three different Old Testament scriptures to help his disciples (and us) grasp the meaning of his bloody death – now only hours away.

'Blood of the covenant'

This comes from Exodus 24:8, when God made his covenant with Israel at Mount Sinai. There were sacrifices, the reading of God's law, a covenant commitment, the sprinkling of blood and then a meal with God. This sealed the relationship between God and his people after the exodus. God had redeemed them; now they belonged to him. So what Jesus means is, '*My* blood, which will be poured out in sacrifice, seals the relationship between you and God. You and all my future disciples will be mine for ever in covenant love and commitment. I have redeemed you; you are mine.'

. . . 'which is poured out for many'

These words from Isaiah 53:12 recall the Servant of the Lord portrayed in that chapter. The Servant will suffer and die – yet not for his own sins, but for *ours*.

> He was pierced for *our* transgressions,
>   he was crushed for *our* iniquities;
> the punishment that brought *us* peace was on him,
>   and by his wounds *we* are healed.
> (Isaiah 53:5)

But after his unjust death, God will vindicate and exalt his Servant. Why? 'Because he *poured out* his life unto death . . . for he bore the sin of *many*' (Isaiah 53:12). So Jesus identifies himself as the obedient Servant of the Lord. And today we can rejoice that his vicarious death has brought us resurrection life with him, for ever.

'for the forgiveness of sins'

The other Gospels (and some manuscripts of Matthew) quote Jesus as saying 'blood of the *new covenant*'. And that takes us to Jeremiah 31:33–34. God promised that there would be a permanently restored relationship with his people. And the bottom line of that promise was, 'I will forgive their wickedness and will remember their sins no more.' So Jesus is saying, 'That promise will be fulfilled and total forgiveness will be made possible through my atoning death.'

I imagine that Jesus probably explained further why he quoted these scriptures as the meal with his disciples went on. But can you hear what he was saying? Before the sun would set the next day, he would be executed as a criminal, his body broken and his blood shed. But his death would be the redeeming sacrifice, whose benefits we and all his disciples would share just as we share the bread and wine. Those three scriptures in one cup mean that, through his blood, we too are redeemed from slavery to sin and death, forgiven our sins and brought into new covenant relationship with God in the bonds of love for ever.

Christ, our Passover lamb, has been sacrificed. Therefore let us keep the Festival . . .
(1 Corinthians 5:7–8)

Friday
Three temptations on the cross

Bible reading: Luke 23:32–43

'Save yourself!'

Three times, as he hung on the cross, Jesus heard those words shouted at him with jeering mockery. Three times those shouts must have tested his resolve, for he knew that he *could* have saved himself, with legions of angels at his command (Matthew 26:53). Yet three times he resisted – just as he had done in the wilderness at the very start of his earthly ministry. Luke probably means us to make that connection (Luke 4:1–13).

The tactics were the same: 'If you are the Son of God . . .' 'If you are the Messiah . . .' 'If you are the king of the Jews.' Back then, the devil had tried three times to tempt Jesus to avoid the path of suffering and death, and choose some alternative way to glory. And even now, at the cross itself, the devil makes three last desperate attempts. If only he could get Jesus to save *himself*, then Jesus's whole mission to save *the world* would be lost. So he speaks through three different people, who all make the same taunt, but mean it in different ways.

But there is massive irony between what they *think* they are saying and the actual *truth* of the situation. Take a look at each of them in turn.

The religious rulers (verse 35)

Their mockery was a rejection of the claims of Jesus to be God's Messiah, God's chosen One, the Saviour king. How could he save anybody else if he couldn't save himself? Yet, of course, their words state exactly who Jesus was. So they both state the truth and reject the truth in the same breath.

The Roman soldiers (verses 36–38)

Their mockery was a rejection of the charge against Jesus: that he was supposed to be the 'king of the Jews'. But that's ridiculous! 'What kind of king are you up there, with thorns for your crown and a cross for your throne?' And yet those words above his head, the butt of their laughter, were a bald statement of the truth.

The resistance fighter (verse 39)

His mockery was a rejection of Jesus' failure to be the kind of messianic leader that he and his band of brigands wanted, to lead them in rebellion against Rome. 'You should have joined us if you'd been a real messiah. Well, here's your last chance. Save yourself and us and we'll slaughter these Romans together! Ha, ha! As if . . .'

But Jesus refused to save himself. Not because he couldn't (as all three voices sneeringly thought), but because *he chose not to*. Jesus resisted these three last temptations, and, as he did so, we see two astonishing paradoxes.

The paradox of power

Can you detect the different kinds of human power alluded to in those three voices? Look at the religious establishment in its crushing self-righteousness, imperial military force in its callous brutality and nationalistic fanaticism with its raw violence. Horrid human power in all its cruelty. But who was exercising real power at that very moment? The powerless one on the middle cross. The paradox is that, in choosing to surrender his life in utter powerlessness, Jesus was exercising *the loving power of God* through which, alone, all the powers of human and satanic evil would be defeated and ultimately destroyed.

Rejoice today that the 'weakness' of the cross was the power of God!

The paradox of salvation

'Save yourself *and us*' was the third mocking insult. But, of course, that was precisely what Jesus *could not do*. Can you see? He could not *both* save himself *and* save us.

- *Either* he could save himself, and he knew it, with that army of angels at the ready. But, if he had saved himself, he could not have saved us through his atoning death for our sin.
- *Or* he could choose to save us (which was the very purpose of his coming), but in that case he could not save himself. So Jesus *chose* to die, *chose* to stay on the cross and endure the agony, the shame and the outer darkness of separation between Father and Son, so that we might be saved.

No wonder we sing,

'Bearing shame and scoffing rude,
in my place condemned he stood.
Sealed my pardon with his blood.
Hallelujah! what a Saviour!'
(From Philip P. Bliss, 'Man of Sorrows, What a Name, 1875)

Saturday
Three completions in one word

Bible reading: John 19:28–30

Are you planning to attend a three-hour meditation on Good Friday? Perhaps the speaker will reflect on the seven sayings of Jesus from the cross.

John records for us two of the best-known: 'I thirst' and 'It is finished'. But the way he does so takes us right inside the mind of Jesus at that moment. How did John know what Jesus was thinking on the cross? I suppose it must have been from a conversation with Jesus after his resurrection.

Death as an achievement?

Shouldn't we be surprised that John paints the whole scene at this moment as one of *achievement*? The clue lies in John's choice of three words, the first and last of which are identical in Greek and the middle one very similar:

- Everything had now been *finished.*
- So that Scripture would be *fulfilled.*
- 'It is *finished.*'

This can't be accidental. John is making a point. And his point is that Jesus spoke these words (a) because of what he *knew* (that all things were completed) and (b) because of what he *intended* (to fulfil Scripture). Jesus was at the very point of death, and yet he was still utterly in control of his thoughts and his words.

Everything had now been finished . . .

Or, rather, completed. Jesus knew that nothing could now stand in the way of his death. Now you might think this is rather obvious for anybody nailed to a cross: 'This is the end. I'm going to die.' Well, yes. But, you see, it was only because Jesus had been utterly *determined* to die that he had reached this point of no return. So much had conspired to *stop* him getting to this moment of inevitable death.

Think back over the story. Herod tried to kill him as an infant, which was not the atoning death God had planned. The devil tried to divert him in the wilderness. Peter tried to dissuade him at Caesarea Philippi. His own mother and family tried to get him to come home and be sensible. He himself struggled with the prospect in Gethsemane. Pilate wanted to release him. Everybody was taunting him, even on the cross, to save himself, as we saw yesterday. But Jesus won the final victory. He knew what he had come to do, to 'give his life as a ransom for many' (Mark 10:45).

It was God's purpose, and his own purpose, for him to reach this point. All is completed. Nothing can stop him any longer from giving his life for us. And, *knowing that*, Jesus returns again to the Scriptures that have guided his life and now fill his dying consciousness.

So that Scripture would be fulfilled . . .

Jesus gasps, *'I am thirsty.'* Well of course he was! Rapid dehydration was part of the torture of crucifixion. But Jesus wets his lips so that he can speak words to fulfil the Scriptures. But which piece of scripture? Possibly Psalm 69:19–21. But more likely, since he had already quoted the first verse of Psalm 22 ('My God, my God, why have you forsaken me?'), Jesus now remembers verse 15: 'My strength is dried up like a potsherd, and my tongue sticks to the roof of my mouth; you lay me in the dust of death.' And John has already sensed an echo of that psalm in the soldiers' gambling for Jesus' clothing (John 19:24).

But don't imagine that this is merely another 'prediction coming true' – that's far too shallow. This is the deep resonance in the mind of Jesus with the Scriptures as a whole that had governed his every waking moment and now fill his dying breaths.

Why do you think Psalm 22 is filling the consciousness of Jesus on the cross? Because he found in *both halves* of the psalm words that expressed on the one hand the depth of his suffering (verses 1–18), and, on the other hand, the breadth of his faith and hope in God (verses 19–31). Jesus died in agony, but he did not die in despair. Jesus suffered separation from his Father, but he knew that God would not ultimately abandon him. Jesus endured the mockery of evil men so that sinners in every nation would seek the Lord and praise him (verse 27). Jesus trusted in God, and God *did* deliver him – not *from* the cross, but *through* the cross in the glorious vindication of Easter Day.

'It is finished'

Some scholars suggest that Jesus' final cry of triumph reflects the very last line of Psalm 22 – 'He has done it!' God has done it! Through Jesus! Through his death on the cross! This was the third and ultimate completion that John heard from the mouth of Jesus.

Look again at those six bullet points in the Introduction (p. 2) where I summarized all that God has accomplished through the cross of Christ. God planned it. God revealed it in the Scriptures. Jesus accomplished it all. So you and I can rejoice and rest assured in that great completion. Amazing! And in the coming six weeks, we will explore it all together.

Week 1
EVIL DEFEATED

Sunday
The conquest of evil in six acts

The seventy-two returned with joy and said, 'Lord, even the demons submit to us in your name.' He replied, 'I saw Satan fall like lightning from heaven ... However, do not rejoice that the spirits submit to you, but rejoice that your names are written in heaven.'
(Luke 10:17–20)

The reason the Son of God appeared was to destroy the devil's work.
(1 John 3:8)

How did God, through Christ, win the victory over [the devil]? The conquest is depicted in Scripture as unfolding in six stages, although the decisive defeat of Satan took place at the cross.

Stage one is *the conquest predicted*. The first prediction was given by God himself in the Garden of Eden as part of his judgment on the serpent: 'And I will put enmity between you and the woman, and between your offspring and hers; he will crush your head, and you will strike his heel' (Gen. 3:15). We identify the woman's seed as the Messiah, through whom God's rule of righteousness will be established and the rule of evil eradicated ...

The second stage was *the conquest begun* in the ministry of Jesus. Recognizing him as his future conqueror, Satan made many different attempts to get rid of him, for example, through Herod's murder of the Bethlehem children, through the wilderness temptations to avoid the way of the cross, [etc.] ... But Jesus was determined to fulfil what had been written of him. He announced that through him, God's kingdom had come upon that very generation, and that his mighty works were visible evidence of it. We see his kingdom advancing and Satan's retreating before it, as demons are dismissed, sicknesses are healed and disordered nature itself acknowledges its Lord . . .

The third and decisive stage [was] *the conquest achieved*, at the cross. Three times, according to John, Jesus referred to . . . 'the prince of this world', adding that he was about to 'come' (i.e. to launch his last offensive), but would be 'driven out' and 'condemned' (Jn. 12:31; 14:30; 16:11). He was evidently anticipating that at the time of his death the final contest would take place, in which the powers of darkness would be routed. It was by his death that he would 'destroy him who holds the power of death – that is, the devil – 'and so set his captives free' (Heb. 2:14–15). Perhaps the most important New Testament passage in which the victory of Christ is set forth is Colossians 2:13–15 . . .

Fourthly, the resurrection was *the conquest confirmed and announced*. We are not to regard the cross as defeat and the resurrection as victory. Rather, the cross was the victory won, and the resurrection was victory endorsed, proclaimed and demonstrated. 'It was impossible for death to keep its hold on him', because death had already been defeated. The evil principalities and powers, which had been deprived of their weapons and their dignity at the cross, were in consequence put under his feet and made subject to him (Acts 2:24; Eph. 1:20–23; 1 Pet. 3:22) . . .

Fifthly, *the conquest is extended* as the church goes out on its mission, in the power of the Spirit, to preach Christ crucified as Lord, and to summon people to repent and believe in him. In every true conversion there is a turning not only from sin to Christ, but 'from darkness to light', 'from the power of Satan to God' and 'from idols to serve the living and true God'; there is also a rescue 'from the dominion of darkness . . . into the kingdom of the Son God loves' (Acts 26:18; 1 Thess. 1:9; Col. 1:13). So every Christian conversion involves a power encounter in which the devil is obliged to relax his hold on somebody's life and the superior power of Christ is demonstrated.

Sixthly, we are looking forward to *the conquest consummated* at the Parousia. The interim between the two advents is to be filled with the church's mission. The Lord's Anointed is already reigning, but he is also waiting until his enemies become his footstool for his feet. On that day every knee will bow to him and every tongue confess him Lord. The devil will be thrown into the lake of fire, where death and Hades will join him. For the last enemy to be destroyed is death. Then, when all evil dominion, authority and power have been destroyed, the Son will hand over the kingdom to the Father, and he will be all in all (Ps. 110:1; Phil. 2:9–11; Rev. 20:10, 14; 1 Cor. 15:24–28).

John Stott, *The Cross of Christ*, pp. 269–275

Monday
Evil invades – God promises

Bible reading: Genesis 3:1–15

Last week, after Ash Wednesday, we focused each day on some aspect of the cross. But how and why did we ever reach that point? Why was the cross necessary? Where did it all start?

This week we go back to the very beginning of the story. Well, nearly the beginning, for, of course, the Bible story begins with God's good creation and the part God intended for us to play within it. We were created to love God and one another and, as the image of God, to steward and care for God's creation. But instead, in the profound simplicity of today's reading, we chose a different way – disastrously. We chose the path of evil and sin.

Did we fall or were we pushed?

Genesis 3 is usually called the story of 'the fall'. But don't you think that's an inadequate word for what happened? I mean, we didn't just *accidentally* slip and fall, did we? No, quite deliberately, we *chose* to distrust God's goodness, we chose to disregard God's warnings, we chose to disobey God's instructions. 'Rebellion' would be a better word. Or, in the story's own terms, we decided that we would choose for ourselves what constitutes 'good and evil' – rather than trusting God to determine that for us. And what a mess we have made of the moral autonomy we grabbed. The first things it brought us were both fear in the presence of God and shame in the presence of one another. And a lot worse would follow in the coming chapters.

But were we 'pushed'? Well, the story shows we were *tempted*, but that's not the same thing, is it? Eve's conversation with the serpent shows her acquiescing to the serpent's hints and suggestions, and not rebutting its straight denial of God's warning. Neither she nor Adam was *forced* to disobey God. It was their freely chosen act.

The radical invasion of sin

In that one act, a mysterious force of evil found an entry point into human life and history. Sin invaded every dimension of the human person. Look how the simplicity of the story conceals great insights.

- *Spiritually*, Eve's trusting relationship with God is already fracturing.
- *Mentally*, she is using God-given powers (verse 6: rationality, aesthetic appreciation, desire for wisdom – all good things in themselves) in a direction that God had prohibited.
- *Physically*, she 'took . . . and ate' – actions within the created world.
- *Relationally*, she shared her sinful act with her husband (who was 'with her', please note, gentlemen).

So sin totally infects the individual person. But when you read the next few chapters, it gets much worse, doesn't it? There are jealousy, anger and murder between brothers; boasting vengeance; corruption and violence throughout society, and the rampant arrogance of the human race. Evil and sin escalate, engulfing individuals, generations, nations and creation itself. The Bible gives us a very radical diagnosis of human sin. Thankfully, God also gives us a Radical Reconciler to deal with the scale of the problem.

The mystery of evil

Genesis 3 does not, however, tell us 'the origin of evil' as such. In fact, I don't think the Bible ever gives a straight answer to the question, 'Where did evil come from?' We are not told what the serpent was, why it was 'more cunning' or how it could talk. All we can say is that it just seems completely out of place – an intruder. Later, of course, the Bible does identify it with Satan. But in Genesis all we know is that the enticement of evil doesn't come from God, or indeed from within humans themselves, originally. A mysterious evil presence and power is at work – lying, deceptive and clearly hostile to God. Where, what, why, how – all these are left unanswered. Presumably, God thinks, 'That is something you don't need to know.'

God's plan is not to *explain* evil, but ultimately to *overcome and destroy* it. And that is why Genesis 3:15 is so important. God's promise is that evil, embodied here in the serpent, will not have the last word, but will finally be crushed. That is such good news. A serpent's-head-crusher will come! A human son of Eve. We rejoice to know that he has indeed come, and won that victory for us. Truly, the gospel begins in Genesis.

Take a moment to identify some of the spiritual, mental, physical and relational dimensions of sin in your own life. Then give thanks that the power of evil that lies behind them has been defeated by Christ, and praise God that we look forward to the complete liberation that he promises.

Tuesday
'The Lord is a warrior'[1]

Bible reading: Exodus 15:1–18

Do you find it hard to read this Song of Moses and Miriam without a twinge of pity for the Egyptian charioteers? And what about those poor horses? Indeed, to get the sheer horror of it all, read 14:23–28.

So why am I inflicting this story, and this seemingly heartless triumphant song, on your devotions today? Because the Bible will not allow us to underestimate the terrible weight of evil in the world, and its tragic consequences. For, let's be clear, it was the defiant arrogance and incorrigible wickedness of their boss – the Pharaoh – that sent those elite troops and their horses to their watery destruction.

A classic case of evil

Before we stand in judgment on Exodus 15, we need to read Exodus 1 and 5, and see the reasons why the Pharaoh stood under God's judgment. For a prolonged period, and with only a politically motivated and specious excuse, he had inflicted a reign of terror on an immigrant ethnic minority within his country. Doesn't it all sound familiar and modern? The Hebrews were subjected to economic exploitation (slave labour), to social subversion and invasion of their family life, and eventually to state-sponsored genocide. And throughout the long chapters of the conflict between the Pharaoh and Israel's God, he resists and rejects every effort and offer to change course – including from his own government

---

1 Not 'a worrier' (as a student of mine once hastily wrote while quoting this verse in an exam) – although I imagine that we do give him plenty to worry about.

advisors. He hardens his heart repeatedly, until God, as it were, accepts and accelerates his chosen path towards irreversible judgment. Feel sympathy if you like for doomed soldiers and horses, but the text shows none for the Pharaoh.

The Pharaoh is a kind of archetype of defiant human evil shaking its fist against God. And it is typical of such evil that, when God finally acts to defeat and destroy it, it drags down so much of human and creaturely life in its wake. The power and the cost of evil are frightening. So can we understand, then, why the *defeat* of murderous evil is such good news that it generates this exhilarating and grateful song? This is the relief and joy that evil has been defeated and those who were oppressed and threatened have been liberated. If you'd been an Israelite that morning after the terror and horror of the night before, would you have just quietly muttered, 'Oh, that's a bit of a relief'? (No, didn't think so.)

Rejoicing but not gloating

This song, then, is not gloating over the lives lost, but rejoicing in the lives saved. For as Ezekiel will later tell us, in the wake of God's terrible judgment on his own people for their wickedness, 'As surely as I live, declares the Sovereign Lord, I take no pleasure in the death of the wicked, but rather that they turn from their ways and live. Turn! Turn from your evil ways! Why will you die, people of Israel?' (Ezekiel. 33:11). There is an ancient Jewish tradition that, as the sea returned and the Egyptian charioteers and horses drowned, the angels burst into song. But God rebuked them, saying, 'The work of my hands is perishing, and do you sing?' It was right for Moses and Miriam to celebrate deliverance, but God's judgments bring tears, not joy, to God's heart.

'Deliver us from evil'

You could think of what happened in the sea in Exodus 14 – 15 as a 'signal event' – one of several actually in the Old Testament. That is, it is like a signpost pointing to something beyond and greater than itself, in which God acts both to defeat evil and to save people even in the midst of judgment. What others could you put in that category? The flood (Noah's family); Sodom and Gomorrah (Lot's family); the conquest of Canaan (Rahab's family); the destruction of Jerusalem and the exile (the remnant). All of these point forward, to show us that God will never allow evil to have the last word. He defeated it decisively at the cross, and will destroy it ultimately and totally from the new creation. The plot-line of the whole Bible, really, is the defeat of evil by the living God, and the Pharaoh's downfall is but one graphic episode in the story.

'For yours is the kingdom . . .'

But the good news doesn't stop with evil defeated. Moses and Miriam don't only celebrate how wonderful it was to be liberated from *past* slavery. They look ahead to God's *future* plans for his people (verse 13), and they recognize who really is king – and it isn't the Pharaoh (verses 11, 18)! The *mission* of God and the *reign* of God. Those are the enduring messages of their song. And this is the first clear affirmation of the kingdom of God in the Bible.

Read verse 13 aloud several times, and hear its message lifted above its immediate context here. Here is the whole Bible story in a nutshell! Are you among the people God has redeemed? Then rejoice in God's 'unfailing love', and be reassured that he will lead you, with all God's redeemed people, to the place of God's own dwelling – the new creation (Revelation 21:3).

Wednesday
The finger of God

Bible reading: Luke 11:14–22

'The Lord reigns!'

That was the closing message of yesterday's reading, and it is the resounding message of today's. Yesterday it was the climax of the power encounter between the living God and an arrogant human despot. Today, it is an episode in the climax of the battle between the Son of God and Satan.

I wonder what comes to your mind when you hear the phrase 'the kingdom of God'? Perhaps a mixture of the parables of Jesus? Or an impression of heaven? In the Gospels, however, a key element is spiritual conflict, a cosmic battle. When God comes to reign, evil powers fight back, but are decisively defeated. Jesus may well have had the exodus story in mind as the classic scriptural case of God's victory over evil when he said, 'If I drive out demons by *the finger of God*, then the kingdom of God has come upon you.' For that is what even the Pharaoh's magicians recognized, as the God of the Hebrews struck Egypt again and again. 'This is the finger of God,' they exclaimed (Exodus 8:19)!

Startling proof

And most of the crowd on this occasion thought the same thing. They were 'amazed' (verse 14). Well, there's an understatement, don't you think? Here is a man, afflicted by an evil spirit, who everybody knew could not speak, and Matthew tells us he was blind as well (Matthew 12:22). And Jesus drives out the spirit and liberates the man from his demonic prison of silence and darkness. 'Jesus healed him, so that he could both talk and see,' says Matthew.

Astonished? Of course they were – the man's unchained voice was audible proof of what Jesus had just done. He had overpowered and expelled the powers of evil. Who, then, could Jesus be? The promised Messiah, son of David? The one through whom God's own reign would arrive?

Ridiculous resistance

But for some, that conclusion was threateningly unwelcome, so they came up with their own explanation. 'You think he's doing all this by the power of *God*? That's fake news! Jesus is driving out demons by the power of the king of demons.'

Sorry, what?

Jesus brilliantly debunks the illogical stupidity of such 'alternative facts'. And then he challenges the crowd with the only believable truth. If his power over evil spirits (which was undeniable: the healed man was jabbering away over there with all the excitement of his loosened tongue and shining eyes!) is clear evidence that God is at work (by his finger, Luke, or by his Spirit, Matthew), then there is only one conclusion. The kingdom of God has already come among and upon them. The battle is joined, and Jesus wins. 'The reason the Son of God appeared,' says John, 'was to destroy the devil's work' (1 John 3:8).

'Someone stronger'

And that is exactly what is going on here, and throughout Jesus's earthly ministry. Jesus's comparison is graphic and decisive. Verse 21 portrays Satan gloating over his prisoners. Verse 22 portrays Jesus in combat – attacking and overpowering, depriving Satan of both his power and his plunder.

> Here is the ultimate cosmic war. Jesus and Satan stand toe to toe in battle. The miracles are an audiovisual that Satan's cause is ultimately lost. He can do great damage, as any enemy can; but the die is cast. He will lose. The picture of the 'stronger one' alludes back to [what John the Baptist said in] 3:15–16. The stronger one is the promised Messiah who brings fire and

the Spirit ... Jesus's work means that Satan is no longer in control of the palace.
(Darrell L. Bock, *Luke*, p. 211)

And on the cross, Jesus completed the victory that will ultimately expel Satan from God's universe altogether.

In a cosmic war there are no spectators; everyone lines up on one side or the other. The implication is to be careful which side you choose. The miracles not only make a statement about Jesus' authority; they ask a question about our response (Darrell Bock, on verse 23).

Evil has been defeated by Christ, in his life and his death. But the evil one is still rampant in the world, until his final destruction. Like a roaring lion (1 Peter 5:8).

Take time today deliberately to renounce, reject and resist him. Affirm and celebrate his downfall, renew your allegiance to Christ and rejoice in the victory that Christ won for us. Claim Paul's promise, 'The God of peace will soon crush Satan under your feet' (Romans 16:20). The Lord reigns!

Thursday
God's cosmic triumph

Bible reading: Colossians 2:6–15

Were you, with the crowd, amazed yesterday, as Jesus, by the finger of God, liberated one tongue and one pair of eyes belonging to one man afflicted by one evil spirit? (I hope we never lose our sense of astonishment at familiar Gospel stories.) But there are much larger communities of people afflicted by much wider forces of evil.

Captivity of the mind

Whole cultures can be victims of a captivity of the mind and imagination. Hostile spiritual powers corrupt and infiltrate the social fabric of human life – including political structures and authorities, ideologies, world views, even the way people habitually think and act as 'normal'. Things that are in themselves part of God's good creation, such as our diverse ethnicities and cultures, our sexuality, food and drink, economic activity in the work-place – all of these can be corrupted into idolatries, pervaded by subtle powers of evil.

You'd think, wouldn't you, that Christians should be immune to all that. Haven't we turned from idols to the living God? Haven't we renounced the evil one and all his ways? Well, yes. But we can so easily be sucked back into the world's mindset by the sheer pressure of the culture around us (remember Romans 12:1–2). Or even by religious rules that sound so spiritual, but end up suffocating the life out of us. We don't exhibit any of the Hollywood movie carica-tures of 'demon possession'. But powers of evil that have colonized the world around us shape the way we think.

Stay free!

Paul wants the believers in Colossae to be free from all such bondage. He warns them not to get 'taken captive' by deceptively plausible ideas that are merely human, worldly and idolatrous (verse 8). In Paul's world, that would have included the cultural seduction of Roman power and civilization, and the religious attraction of forms of Judaism that had not accepted Jesus as Messiah. What do you think might fit that description in the world around us these days?

So how does Paul fight back against such powerful forces? He confronts them with the cross! And he reminds the Colossians of the victory God accomplished there.

From death to life (verses 12–13a)

Paul sees baptism as a symbol of how we share Christ's death and resurrection. His story is our story. The first half of verse 13 describes the Gentile Colossians ('you') from a Jewish point of view – 'dead in sins … and uncircumcision'. Paul expands that vividly in Ephesians 2:11–12. But, like the Prodigal Son, God has brought the dead to life, as alive as Christ himself is.

From sin to forgiveness (verses 13b–14)

But death is the penalty for sin (as we have known since the Garden of Eden). So, to give us life out of death, God must deal with sin. And he has, says Paul triumphantly! He has forgiven *us* (Paul knows that he and his fellow Jews are as much sinners in need of forgiveness as the Gentiles) all our sins. How? In a vivid metaphor, Paul sees our sin as a massive debt. But God chooses to cancel this debt and nail the accusing document to the cross itself. Which means that God, in Christ, chose to pay the debt himself; the cross was the cost to God of our forgiveness.

From captivity to freedom (verse 15)

But sin and death were not the only powers that God dealt with at the cross. All 'powers and authorities' that deceive and enslave, whether working through political and economic structures, or religious systems, or spiritual idolatries, or human ideologies and rules (as in verse 8 and verses 16–23), have been exposed and disarmed at the cross. Christ's apparent defeat was the place of his glorious triumph. And by his victory we are set free.

> Anyone looking at the cross of Jesus with a normal understanding of the first-century world would think: the rulers and authorities stripped him naked and celebrated a public triumph over him. That's what they normally did to such people.
>
> Now blink, rub your eyes and read verse 15 again. On the cross, Paul declares, *God* was stripping the armour off *the rulers and authorities*! Yes: *he* was holding *them* up to public contempt! God was celebrating *his* triumph over the principalities and powers, the very powers that thought it was the other way round. Paul never gets tired of relishing the glorious paradox of the cross: God's weakness overcoming human strength.
>
> (Tom Wright, *Paul for Everyone: The Prison Letters*, pp. 170–171; italics original)

Three questions: where do you see the relevance of Paul's warning (verse 8) in your own habits of thought and life, and within your Christian community? What would it mean to discern and confront the subtle infiltration of evil powers into our day-to-day assumptions from the world around us? And what will it mean to regard them, instead, in the light of Christ's triumph on the cross, as 'a ragged and defeated rabble'?

Friday
There's a war on

Bible reading: Ephesians 6:10–17

'The Lord is a warrior'

Do you remember that line from Tuesday's reflection on the Song of Moses and Miriam (Exodus 15:3)? We may not relish the military imagery, but it's the spiritual truth that counts. Through the whole Bible, God is engaged in a mighty cosmic battle against the powers of evil, spiritual and human. So the metaphor of God himself as a warrior comes naturally – a warrior fighting to overcome evil and defeat all that opposes his good and loving purposes for creation and human life.

And, like a human soldier, God clothes himself with the right equipment. You've probably heard preachers say that Paul draws his picture of the armour of God from the Roman soldier he might have been chained to in prison. Very possibly. But, actually, most of the meanings Paul gives to each piece come from the Old Testament – his Scriptures. And they describe either God himself or the coming Messiah (you can check the relevant references below in a moment).

So, you see, when Paul says 'the full armour *of God*', he doesn't just mean bits of equipment that God hands out like army kit. No, this is what God himself wears! We fight under the protection of the character and attributes of God himself, for he is the God of truth, righteousness, peace, faithfulness, salvation and Spirit-inspired word. And that's what we need (or rather, *who* we need), to stand firm in the battle.

'Don't you know there's a war on?'

That's what people used to say to one another in Britain during the Second World War, apparently, if somebody was complaining or shirking their duties or just talking too loosely. When there's a war on, everybody needs to be watchful and prepared to put up with hardships and suffering.

Maybe Paul is saying that to the Ephesians: 'Don't you know there's a war on?' Except that in this war, none of us is a civilian. We are all soldiers on active duty because the whole church is on the front line of God's cosmic battle. And the enemies of God and the church are legion. Now, of course, Paul suffered at the hands of 'flesh-and-blood' human opponents – as the church still does today. But Paul knew that the struggle goes on at a higher level altogether, with his comprehensive list of 'the spiritual forces of evil'. They are a defeated enemy (as we saw yesterday), but they still fight venomously with 'flaming arrows' against God and his people.

The full armour of God

The complete picture portrays aspects of God himself, of God's Messiah and of the gospel. What greater protection do you need? There isn't any! The references show what scriptures Paul may have got his ideas from. (They're worth a quick look.)

- *The belt of truth* (Isaiah 11:5 – the Messiah wears a belt of righteousness, but the whole context speaks of his mission of true judgment and governance). The truth of the gospel holds everything together in Christian life and warfare.
- *The breastplate of righteousness* (Isaiah 59:17). Paul may be thinking of the saving righteous acts of God (its frequent meaning in the Old Testament), or the righteousness in which we stand through faith in Christ. But there is spiritual protection also in the righteous integrity of life that Paul calls for (4:24; 5:8–9). Living right makes the devil's work harder.
- *The shoes of the gospel of peace* (Isaiah 52:7). There's nothing 'beautiful' about feet, until they are wearing the running shoes

of the messengers of the good news of God's peace for those who need to hear it (as Paul quotes in Romans 10:14–15).

- *The shield of faith* (Psalms 18:35; 28:7, etc.). The psalmists put their faith in God, to be their shield against all kinds of nasty attacks. So too can we.
- *The helmet of salvation* (Isaiah 59:17). 'The LORD is my light and my salvation – whom shall I fear?' (Psalm 27:1). Enough said.
- *The sword of the Spirit – the word of God* (Isaiah 11:4b; 49:2). Jesus used the Scriptures to resist the temptations of the devil. And so can we. Fight back!

Did *you* know that there's a war on? To be honest, it is very easy to forget the reality of spiritual warfare in the 'ordinariness' of so much Christian daily life. Could it be that our lives are so little threat to the devil and his works that he sees no point in attacking us? But when he does? Ah, then, we need the protection and defence of God's own armour. Get it on you! 'Put on the gospel armour / each piece put on with prayer.' Verse 13 is a command, not a suggestion.

Saturday
Hallelujah!

Bible reading: Revelation 18:1–3; 18:20 – 19:9

The war drags on

On D-Day, 6 June 1944, with the Allied invasion of Normandy, the decisive victory of the Second World War began. And by September that year, they had coined the term 'VE Day'; 'Victory in Europe' was assured and eagerly anticipated. But the war went on for eleven more months of bloody fighting, and VE Day did not actually arrive until 8 May 1945.

In the three years of Jesus' earthly ministry, and supremely at the cross, God in Christ won the decisive victory over all the forces of evil. But the end of the cosmic war lies ahead of us still – assured and eagerly anticipated, even in the midst of the suffering and persecution and battles that God's people endure in this interim period between the first Easter and the Lord's return.

Throughout this week, I hope you have spotted that we have traced the story of God's defeat of evil from Genesis to Revelation, from the serpent's injection of evil into human life and history and God's promise that the serpent itself would be crushed (Genesis 3), right through to the rejoicing of all creation in God's victory (Revelation 19). What a story! What a plot! What a climactic ending (and new beginning too)!

'Rejoice, you people of God!' (Revelation 18:20)

Just as the Song of Moses and Miriam celebrated the downfall of the Pharaoh, so Revelation 19 answers the threefold call of 18:20 to rejoice over the downfall of Babylon. Now you'll be aware, I'm sure, that in the Old Testament Babylon was an actual city, the centre of an empire that rose to power under Nebuchadnezzar and ruled the Middle East for about seventy years, in the days of Jeremiah and Ezekiel, roughly from 605 to 538 BC. But 'Babylon' then became a symbolic word, a code name for all the evil and tyrannical regimes, ancient and modern, that have blighted, exploited and destroyed countless human lives throughout history. And it is in that sense that Revelation condemns 'Babylon'. Of course, John's readers in his day would have had no difficulty recognizing the Roman Empire in his portrayal. But the evils he describes in chapter 18 (read the whole chapter) could apply to many a regime that has perpetrated social, political and economic injustice and oppression, along with the vicious persecution of God's people.

'Fallen is Babylon the Great!'

Indeed, Babylon by this stage of the book of Revelation has come to stand for the whole world of human and satanic rebellion ranged against God and God's people – arrogant, boastful, voraciously greedy, devouring and destructive of human life and created resources.

But not for ever! God will bring her down, and her destruction will be decisive, permanent, eternal (did you spot the repeated 'never again' litany of 18:21–24?). Maybe you find the language of these chapters too graphic and brutal. But remember that God's final judgment is part of the biblical gospel. It is *good* news that God will not let evil have the last word. He promised to crush the serpent's head. He triumphed over evil powers at the cross. And he will ultimately defeat and destroy Satan's whole regime and all that goes with it. God is the Judge of all the earth who will do what is right (Genesis 18:25; Revelation 18:8, 20; 19:1). God will put all things right before he makes all things new (21:5).

Let the party begin!

And so the hallelujahs ring out in chapter 19, to usher in the greatest party of all time – the wedding feast of the Lamb (19:7–8). Christ will be united with his bride, and she herself will be utterly cleansed, pure and holy, gorgeously beautiful (21:2) and eternally safe.

That's us, by the way. We're all invited (19:9). Don't you just love how God ends this vast epic narrative that we call our Bible in this way? The lover gets his girl. The bridegroom embraces his bride. All the rivals and villains are ousted. God makes his new home with his people (21:3). And (in a way that will be no fairy tale but gloriously true) 'they all lived happily ever after'.

What battles with evil realities are you facing today? Or maybe you are grieved at the escalating suffering of so many Christian believers under horrendous attack around the world. Pray for endurance, for yourself and for them. For the end will come. Evil will be defeated. The Lamb wins. Hallelujah!

The victory is ours!
For us in might came forth the mighty One;
For us the fight he fought, the triumph won;
The victory is ours!
(Horatius Bonar, 'Blessèd Be God, Our God', 1883)

Week 2

DEATH DESTROYED

Sunday
Freed from the fear of death

But if it is preached that Christ has been raised from the dead, how can some of you say that there is no resurrection of the dead? If there is no resurrection of the dead, then not even Christ has been raised. And if Christ has not been raised, our preaching is useless and so is your faith. More than that, we are then found to be false witnesses about God, for we have testified about God that he raised Christ from the dead. But he did not raise him if in fact the dead are not raised. For if the dead are not raised, then Christ has not been raised either. And if Christ has not been raised, your faith is futile; you are still in your sins. Then those also who have fallen asleep in Christ are lost. If only for this life we have hope in Christ, we are of all people most to be pitied.

But Christ has indeed been raised from the dead, the firstfruits of those who have fallen asleep. For since death came through a man, the resurrection of the dead comes also through a man. For as in Adam all die, so in Christ all will be made alive. But each in turn: Christ, the firstfruits; then, when he comes, those who belong to him. Then the end will come, when he hands over the kingdom to God the Father after he has destroyed all dominion, authority and power. For he must reign until he has put all his enemies under his feet. The last enemy to be destroyed is death . . .

'Death has been swallowed up in victory.'

'Where, O death, is your victory?
    Where, O death, is your sting?'

The sting of death is sin, and the power of sin is the law. But thanks be to God! He gives us the victory through our Lord Jesus Christ.

Therefore, my dear brothers and sisters, stand firm. Let nothing move you. Always give yourselves fully to the work of the Lord, because you know that your labour in the Lord is not in vain.
(1 Cor. 15:12–26, 54–58)

Through Christ we are no longer under the tyranny of death . . . Jesus Christ is able to set free even those who all their lives have been 'held in slavery by their fear of death'. This because by his own death he has 'destroyed' (deprived of power) 'him who holds the power of death – that is, the devil' (Heb. 2:14).

Jesus Christ has not only dethroned the devil, but dealt with sin. In fact, it is by dealing with sin that he has dealt with death. For sin is the 'sting' of death, the main reason why death is painful and poisonous. It is sin which causes death, and which after death will bring the judgment. Hence our fear of it. But Christ has died for our sins and taken them away. With great disdain, therefore, Paul likens death to a scorpion whose sting has been drawn, and to a military conqueror whose power has been broken. Now that we are forgiven, death can harm us no longer. So the apostle shouts defiantly: 'Where, O death, is your victory? Where, O death, is your sting?' There is of course no reply. So, he shouts again, this time in triumph, not disdain: 'Thanks be to God! He gives us the victory through our Lord Jesus Christ' (1 Cor. 15:55–57).

What, then, should be the Christian's attitude to death? It is still an enemy, unnatural, unpleasant, undignified – in fact 'the last enemy to be destroyed'. Yet, it is a defeated enemy. Because Christ has taken away our sins, death has lost its power to harm and therefore to terrify. Jesus summed it up in one of his greatest affirmations: 'I am the resurrection and the life. He who believes in me will live, even though he dies; and whoever lives and believes in me will never die' (1 Cor. 15:26; Jn. 11:25–26). That is, Jesus is the resurrection of believers who die, and the life of believers who live.

41

His promise to the former is 'you will live', meaning not just that you will survive, but that you will be resurrected. His promise to the latter is 'you will never die', meaning not that you will escape death, but that death will prove to be a trivial episode, a transition to fullness of life . . .

This is the victory of Christ into which he allows us to enter.

John Stott, *The Cross of Christ*, pp. 283–286

Monday
Death mocks life

Bible reading: Ecclesiastes 3:9–22; 9:1–10

Aren't you glad, after today's depressing reading, that Lent will end in the glory of Easter Day? Don't you wish that you could share yesterday's reading, and John Stott's reflections, with the writer of Ecclesiastes, just to cheer him up? Nevertheless, even if the resurrection is the ultimate answer (which he could not yet know), we must still let him challenge us with the ruthless honesty of his questions. Our culture tends to avoid thinking or talking about death. Ecclesiastes won't let us get away with that, so neither will I!

The big question

The whole book of Ecclesiastes is a journey, a quest, by someone called Qoheleth ('the Teacher', NIV), to see if he can find an answer to 'the meaning of life, the universe and everything'. Basically, here is the controlling question he asks: 'What do we gain from all the work we have to do in life?' (1:3 and 3:9). And, since work is an essential part of the way God created us to live, his question boils down to: '*What's the point of life itself?*' Does it have any ultimate meaning? Well, how would *you* answer him?

The big gift

Now the Teacher knows that life itself is good. In fact, he says so emphatically no fewer than seven times in this book.[1] When he says 'there is nothing better' for people than to enjoy the blessings of

---

1   Ecclesiastes 2:24–25; 3:12–13; 3:22; 5:18–20; 8:15; 9:7–10; 11:7–9.

everyday life (work, sex, marriage, food and drink), he is not being cynical or hedonistic. He means it. These are *good gifts* from the God of Genesis 1 – 2, who declared his whole creation good – very good indeed (3:12–13). And the Teacher has himself explored all of those good things of life – in abundance. *But* . . . even when you add all these things together, do such things, good as they are, hold the key to the meaning of life itself? No. An awful lot of life and work seems futile, fickle and transient – actually pretty *meaningless* (his favourite word) when you stop to think about it (and he has done, very hard; just skim through 2:12–23).

The big joke?

And the *most* meaningless thing about life is . . . death. Maybe you've heard the grim saying, or seen the graffiti, *'Life sucks. Then you die.'* That gets (most of) Ecclesiastes down to five words. I can see the Teacher sadly nodding his head. Or, as Marilyn Duckworth put it (beloved, I'm told, of medical professionals), 'Life is a sexually transmitted terminal disease' (*Disorderly Conduct*, p. 160).

The Teacher keeps coming back to the baffling, inexplicable mockery that death seems to make of life. Of course, it's better to be wise than foolish. But when you're dead, will it matter (2:13–14)? Of course, it's better to be a human than an animal, but we'll all end up just as dead (3:19–20). Of course, we ought to be good and religious, but can we be sure our destiny will be any different from those who aren't (9:1–3)? Of course, you may protest, it is better at least to be alive than dead. Sure, but only because while you're alive you know you're going to die, whereas the dead know nothing at all (9:4–5). Death makes a macabre joke out of everything we have lived for. We're leaving the table. We're out of the game (9:6).

The big tension

It's relentless. It's poignant. It's disturbing. But above all, it's honest. Honest, that is, as far as the Teacher could see. For what he is describing is the reality of our Genesis 3 world – the world where God told us that death would be the effect of our sin, life would become toil and sweat, and dust would be our destiny. The Teacher forces us to look *that* world full in the face, even while he holds on, with great effort, to the truth he knows from Genesis 1 – 2. That is the unresolved tension of the whole book. Life is good. Death is ghastly.

But it is this very tension that drives us to the cross and resurrection of Christ. If only the Teacher could have known what we know! It would not change the miserable facts about death itself. But it assures us that death is *not* the end. Death is no joke. But death will *not* have the last laugh.

> Death, be not proud, though some have called thee
> Mighty and dreadful, for thou art not so;
> For those whom thou think'st thou dost overthrow
> Die not, poor Death, nor yet canst thou kill me.
> . . .
> One short sleep past, we wake eternally
> And death shall be no more; Death, thou shalt die.
> (From John Donne, *Songs and Sonnets*, 1633)

Tuesday
Death invades life

Bible reading: Psalm 88

As if the Teacher wasn't depressing enough yesterday, here I go again, dampening your devotions with possibly the most dark and dreary chapter in the Bible. Why? Because we need to grapple with realities. Lent is the time for preparing for Easter, the greatest reality in history, in which God defeated what we might call the greatest 'anti-reality' in history – death.

Living death?

Like Ecclesiastes, Heman the Ezrahite who wrote this song (if it can be called that) is brutally honest about the reality of what he's going through. It feels to him like a living death. For death is not just something that happens when you die, is it? There are experiences in life that are deathly in a wider sense. Things that suck the life out of you. Things that crush all the joy of living. Things that make you feel you might as well be dead.

Like depression, for instance. I mean the clinical illness of depression (not just occasionally feeling a bit down in the dumps). And that might be the case for you. I don't know, of course, but many of us have a friend or a family member suffering from depression. I know several who battle with it, both within my family and as work colleagues past and present, godly believers every one of them – like our psalmist here. They tell me that, in its worst depths, depression turns life itself to dust. They say that the lowest pit and the lonely darkness of Psalm 88:6 and 18 tell it like it is for them. This psalm speaks to them and for them.

'Darkness is my closest friend'

Psalm 88's closing words blew me away. Here is no hope; there
seems no faith. It is almost blasphemous – God is meant to be
so good that he is our utterly dependable friend. But to claim
that 'darkness is my closest friend' is to appear to reject God.
At the very least, it illustrates a lost confidence in him . . .

So here is the final paradox. Heman the Ezrahite expresses
in prayer to God what it feels like to have no God at all. He
prays in despair and because of his despair. Even though that
seems like the last thing one should do if there is no God at
work. So, to my mind, Psalm 88 is unexpectedly one of the
Bible's most liberating chapters.
(Mark Meynell, *When Darkness Seems My Closest Friend*,
p. 37)

Liberating?

Really? Yes, because of the sheer amazement that such a psalm
should be in our Bible at all, that God would *allow* it to be there. The
psalmist knows that God *does* hear his cry from the depths, even if
a big part of his pain is that it feels as if God *isn't* listening. And in
his opening line, the psalmist still trusts in God's salvation, even
in his desperation and longing and waiting. The emotions are raw
and real: he feels close to the pit of death (verses 1–6); he feels guilty
and under God's wrath (verses 7, 16); he *wants* to praise God for his
wonders, love, faithfulness and righteous acts – but there'll not be
much chance of doing that in the grave (verses 10–12); he feels
utterly rejected in spite of daily prayer (verses 13–14); and this seems
the story of his whole life (verses 15–18). Is it not liberating to know
that the Bible itself gives you freedom to talk that way, to give voice
to such terrible words, if it's the honest truth about how you feel?

On the lips of Jesus?

I wonder if it's liberating in another way also. Can we imagine
a psalm like this giving expression to the depth of suffering that

Jesus endured for us, as he went through the agony of facing death and separation from his Father? We know for certain that Psalm 22 expressed his suffering, since he quoted it. And probably Psalm 69 would have had deep meaning for him too. Try reading Psalm 88 again through the mind and lips of Jesus, and thank God that, if the psalm now or ever expresses your own experience, Jesus has been there too – and has won the victory over such life-invading deathliness.

Psalm 88 may be a prayer from the depths of your own heart today, or for someone you know and love. If so, I'm sorry. But make sure you don't leave it there. I would prescribe praying Psalm 86 immediately afterwards. And then turn from the darkness to the light of Psalm 27. And from deathliness to the cry for life in Psalm 119:153–160 and 169–176.

Wednesday
Death will be swallowed up

Bible reading: Isaiah 25:1–9

Isn't it a relief, after the gloomy readings of the last two days, to come to Isaiah 25:8 and join in the praise of verses 1 and 9? And it would be even more of a relief if you had just read Isaiah 24 (have a glance). For there, the prophet portrays God's future judgment on the whole earth as like a single city suffering total destruction. But, in the midst of God's shattering cosmic judgment, he will protect and save his own people and his own city – symbolized as Mount Zion (24:23). That is what today's reading celebrates in advance.

Salvation in the midst of judgment

There are two reasons for celebration: that God has defeated and destroyed his enemies (verses 2–3), and that God has been a refuge for the poor and needy among his own people (verses 4–5). Isaiah uses two vivid images of urgent danger drawn from his own world. A torrential thunderstorm and flash flood could sweep you and your house away (remember Jesus' story, Matthew 7:26–27?), and relentless desert sun could desiccate you to death. You needed protection from both, and God provides it. The world will be judged; the Lord's own people will be safe.

In Israel's world, when a new king was crowned, or had won some notable victory, he would throw a great party for his people. He would provide food and drink in abundance, and the festivities would last a long time. Put yourself among Isaiah's listeners, who could well remember such a royal party. And the food! A king could be generous. The Lord God will be no less so. Imagine the best feast of richest food and finest wine you could ever enjoy. What God has in store will go way beyond your imagination (verse 6).

A feast for all

But this divine banquet stretches our imagination even further. Can you see the paradox between its very *particular* location ('on this mountain'), and the *universal* size of the invitation list ('for all peoples')? Mount Zion was the heartbeat of Old Testament Israel. But the feast God would provide would be not for Israel alone, but for all peoples and all nations. Isn't that what God promised Abraham (Genesis 12:3)? God's blessing through Israel will extend to the ends of the earth. That is God's mission, and God invites all nations to the party.

But, in another sense, it would be literally at Mount Zion, in Jerusalem (or rather just outside its walls), that God would accomplish the ultimate victory on the cross of Christ. For, as Paul famously said, 'the last enemy to be destroyed is death' (1 Corinthians 15:26). And that is *the* most wonderful of all the 'wonderful things' that God 'planned long ago' (verse 1). For, after all, what would be the point of enjoying a banquet even with God as chef and host if – as Ecclesiastes won't let us forget – death will be the final course? The whole human race can swallow all the food and drink God provides, but in the end death swallows us, doesn't it? That's our universal destiny. *But not for ever!* says God.

The swallower swallowed

In the world around Israel, some cultures were obsessed with death and what lay beyond it. In Egypt, pharaohs would spend their lives and treasure preparing for their afterlife in the world of the dead – an obsession that gave us the pyramids to wonder at. God gave Israel a far, far better revelation to wonder at. Israelites believed from an early stage that their God Yahweh had power over both life and death. Ask Hannah (1 Samuel 2:6). But they could not avoid Ecclesiastes' dark realism that death eventually swallows everybody and everything. And they knew why: God's universal curse and verdict since Genesis 3. Only occasionally did they catch a glimpse of a resurrection hope that lay ahead.[1]

So Isaiah 25:8 is an astonishing outburst of assurance. It's not just that God can deliver us from death. It's not just that God can give us a future beyond death (not that Israel speculated much about that). No, God is going to destroy death itself! That monster that swallows everything? *God himself will swallow it up . . . for ever!* And when death is no more, then God will set about wiping away all the sorrow it has ever caused. The cosmic Lord of heaven, the Judge of all the earth, stooping to dry the tears on all the cheeks of all the faces . . . What gentleness!

Isaiah 25:8 inspires two other scriptures: the triumph of 1 Corinthians 15:54 and the tenderness of Revelation 21:4. Why not finish today by reading them, and then join in the personal and corporate thanksgiving of Isaiah 25:1 and 9 together? Those can be our words too. What God planned from eternity ('long ago'), we will enjoy for eternity. Hallelujah!

---

1 Isaiah 26:19; Daniel 12:2–3, 13.

Thursday
Jesus invades death's kingdom

Bible reading: John 11:1–44

I mean, how long does it take to get from up there on the other side of the River Jordan down to Bethany here? A day or two's walk at most. But he just didn't come, did he? We sent him a message that our brother Lazarus was dangerously ill, but days passed and no sign of Jesus. And then Lazarus died – our precious brother, and a man still in his prime. Mary and I, we were beside ourselves with grief. It felt as if we'd been widowed. The whole village came round to mourn with us and the house was full of people, weeping and wailing.

And still no Jesus, four days later, and Lazarus's body now wrapped and in the tomb. Surely he'd heard the news by now. Didn't he remember how much we loved him, and how much he loved us and our little home? All those times he'd stayed with us and I'd cooked his favourite food . . . And, in fact, I was in the kitchen again when a friend whispered through the little window that Jesus had reached the edge of the village. I rushed off to find him, leaving Mary with the mourners.

'Lord,' I wailed, 'if only you'd come on time, my brother would not have died.' I couldn't help it. I was hurting so much. It wasn't the first time I'd felt cross with him, but this was far, far worse. If only, if only . . .

'Your brother will rise again,' said Jesus, just like the mourners back home were saying again and again to Mary and me, trying to be comforting in the usual way.

'Well, of course I know that, Lord,' I said. 'I know he will rise on the last day in the resurrection of all the dead.' I mean, all of us Jews believe that (well, except those Sadducees). But that's a long time to wait, and we'll *all* be dead by then, and Jesus could have stopped him dying in the first place. My grief was tipping over into anger.

And then Jesus said words I can never forget:

'*I am* the resurrection and the life (he stressed those first two words). The one who believes in me will live, even though they die; and whoever lives by believing in me will never die. Do you believe this?'

It was more than I could take in, but I did say I believed in *him*. I did and do believe he is the Messiah and the Son of God. But I thought, 'Mary needs to hear this. It'll make more sense to her than me; Jesus always did.'

So I hurried back to the house as fast as my skirts would allow and whispered in Mary's ear that Jesus had arrived. She was sitting on the floor where once she'd sat at Jesus feet, but now she leapt up and hurried to where I'd met Jesus, and fell at those same feet right there. A whole crowd of us followed her, just in time to hear her say, 'Lord, if only you'd come on time, my brother would not have died.'

'Er, been there, said that, sister,' I thought, though I had to wait until later to tell Mary what Jesus answered.

Mary was weeping. Everybody else was too. And then I saw Jesus. His chest was heaving with great sobs and his face was crumpling up in pain. But he managed to ask us where the body was, before bursting into tears himself. Did I tell you how much he loved Lazarus? Everybody could tell. But it actually looked as if he was *angry*, not just grieved – somehow angry at death for stealing Lazarus's life.

We got to the tomb and Jesus went straight up to the entrance.

'Take away the stone!' he commanded. It looked as if he was going to march right in there and invade the world of the dead, like confronting death in its own realm – just as he confronted and overcame the evil spirits. But I was horrified. Didn't he know what a body smells like after four days? Well, I told him, but it made no difference.

'Trust me,' he said, 'and you will see the glory of God.' So, I did and I did!

He looked up and prayed. Then he shouted at the top of his voice, 'Lazarus, come out!' And there he was, shuffling out of the darkness, standing right up straight in the sunlight . . . My brother! Alive!

Mary has helped me understand (she's good at explaining things) what Jesus meant. You see, Lazarus is going to die again some day, isn't he, and Mary and I too. But because Jesus *is* the resurrection, and we believe in him, that won't be the end. We shall live! And because Jesus *is* the life, we know we have eternal life already now and will never truly die. Oh, and yes, we know all this because we were there when Jesus himself died on the cross, and we have seen him even more fully raised from the dead than my brother was (but that's another story).

And that nice young John (whom Jesus loved a lot as well, apparently) says he's going to put our story in the book he's writing about Jesus, and end with the very same words that I said to Jesus! Isn't that good of him? John wants you and everybody to believe, like me, that 'Jesus is the Messiah, the Son of God, and that by believing you may have life in his name'.

Friday
Death's power broken

Bible reading: Hebrews 2:9–18

'It's not that I'm afraid to die,' said Woody Allen. 'I just don't want to be there when it happens.' A lot of people would agree with the second half. We don't want to go through the unpredictable and potentially painful process of actually dying. But is the first half of his claim sincere? I don't know, but I doubt it.

Fear of death

Judging from the vast range of cultures and religions, the human race has a pretty universal fear of death. And why not? Life is such a precious thing, and death is such a mysterious intrusion from a realm that scares us simply because it is so unknowable, so beyond our customary control. Of course, there are many wonderfully brave people who overcome the fear of death for the sake of others – a country's armed forces, police, fire-fighters, emergency and rescue services, medical personnel in lethal epidemics and war zones, bomb disposal officers, lifeboat crews . . . But being willing to *face* death is not the same as having no *fear* of death, is it? Good fear makes you careful. No fear at all is foolhardy.

It's a kind of slavery, says our text in Hebrews (verse 15). And we saw at the start of the week that Ecclesiastes would agree. In the midst of this good world and wonderful life, we are imprisoned in the fear of inevitable death. But here's the thing. It's an open prison now! We can walk out free!

Why? Because 'we see Jesus' (verse 9).

We see Jesus

The writer to the Hebrews opens his letter with an overwhelming affirmation of the deity of Jesus Christ, God's Son, exalting him above all the ranks of angels (Hebrews 1). But then we see Jesus as 'lower than the angels for a little while' – that is, as a man. And why did the divine Son of God have to become fully human? The writer summarizes the point of his whole next section thus: 'so that by the grace of God he might taste death for everyone' (verse 9). And then he expands on that same reason at the end in verse 17: 'in order that . . . he might make atonement for the sins of the people.' In short, God became human in order to die a human death, and in that God–man death to deal with the problem of sin that brought death upon us.

Flesh and blood

Can you see, then, the two fundamental points that Hebrews makes in these verses? First of all, we must grasp the full truth of the incarnation. God became wholly one of us in Jesus Christ, subject to our sufferings, our temptations (verse 18) and our mortality. And this was both 'fitting' and necessary. Only God could save us. But God could not save us remotely, from heaven. Only God in flesh and blood (verse 14a) could take our fallen humanity upon himself and redeem us 'from below'.

Battle dress

Then, second, we see Jesus in battle dress, paradoxically but precisely, in his death. Remember God the warrior last week (Exodus 15)? Remember Jesus overpowering the 'strong man' (Luke 11:21–22)? That's the picture Hebrews has in mind, recalling perhaps the same imagery from Isaiah 49:24–25 and 59:15–20. Jesus in his death took on the worst that human and satanic power could inflict upon him – death itself – and won the victory by taking on himself the sin that gives death its sting and power.

I think the NIV is right to translate verse 14 as '*break the power* of him who holds the power of death', rather than 'destroy' (ESV).

The word means to make ineffective, render impotent. Neither the devil nor death were *destroyed* at the cross, right there and then. *But they will be* – when God's victory is completed at the end (1 Corinthians 15:24–26, 54–57). And, in the meantime, the devil's power to imprison us in the fear of death is broken. Death has lost its sting for those liberated by the cross of Christ. The death of Christ spells the ultimate death of death itself.

We should not think that 'the power of death' means that the devil can just kill whomever he wants. Satan is a created being whose power is subject to God's permission and authority. 'The power of death' probably means the power that the fear of death holds over us, which the devil can certainly exploit. And that is what God has delivered us from through the death of Christ.

Jesus the prisoner's fetters breaks,
    And bruises Satan's head;
Pow'r into strengthless souls He speaks,
    And life into the dead.
(From Charles Wesley, *Hymns and Sacred Poems*, 1749)

Saturday
Death's reign ended

Bible reading: Romans 5:12–21

We go back full circle to where we began our week, with Ecclesiastes lamenting the crippling, life-blighting enigma of death. It's all very well, you see, for Dylan Thomas to write his moving poem (much-loved at funerals) 'And death shall have no dominion' (borrowing the words from the Apostle Paul, of course, who was referring to Jesus; Romans 6:9). For the fact is, it does. Death reigns. Genesis 3 proves its truth for approximately two people every second on this planet.

Sin entered; death reigns

And that's where Paul starts in our passage today: in the Garden of Eden. And with the 'one man' through whom sin entered the world, bringing death to all because all sinned. Now Paul starts in verse 12 with 'Just as . . .', but never quite finishes his sentence. He'll do that when he gets to verses 18–21. But his immediate point is that because sin is the universal state of humankind, death is our universal destiny – at whatever point in history you may have lived. Now, by 'death', Paul (and God in Genesis 3) means more than merely physical death. It is the spiritual death of expulsion from God's presence, 'dead in sins', condemned. It is in that sense that Paul repeats himself: 'death *reigned*' (verses 14, 17), 'sin *reigned* in death' (verse 21).

Kingdom language

That's kingdom language, isn't it? Paul portrays sin and death as twin tyrants – and doubtless he would include Satan as well – over a kingdom that enslaves humanity. But what was it Jesus said? 'If I by the finger of God cast out demons, then the *kingdom of God* has come upon you.' And, for Paul, that is the kingdom of grace – God's grace (verse 21). And so, as we have seen all week, the battle is joined, two kingdoms in mortal combat: one, the reign inaugurated by the 'one man' whose disobedience brought sin and death; the other, the victorious reign of the 'One' whose obedience brings righteousness and eternal life.

O loving wisdom of our God!
when all was sin and shame,
a second Adam to the fight
and to the rescue came.

O wisest love! that flesh and blood,
which did in Adam fail,
should strive afresh against the foe,
should strive, and should prevail.
(From John Henry Newman, 'Praise to the Holiest in the Height', 1865)

And where was this victory won?

Our whole week has focused on the death of death through the death of Christ, so you must know the answer! But you might wonder why Paul does not mention the cross in our passage. Well, of course, it is prominent in 5:6–11 and again in chapter 6. But Paul clearly has the cross in mind in the last part of verse 19: 'So also through the obedience of the one man the many will be made righteous.' Paul is echoing Isaiah 53:11, where the Servant of the Lord, in obedience to the will of his God, would by his vicarious death 'justify many'. Likewise, Jesus, as the Servant, became 'obedient to death – even death on a cross!' (Philippians 2:7–8). Christ's obedience here, then, means his willing acceptance of his Father's will, even though the agonizing struggle of Gethsemane. Where Adam rebelled and disobeyed, Jesus the Son and Servant submitted and obeyed.

And where is this reign to be lived out?

Verse 17 is astonishing. We would expect the opposite to the reign of death in the first half of the verse to be that *Christ* would reign – and of course that is true. But Paul says that those who have received God's gifts of grace and righteousness – *we believers* – are the ones who will 'reign in life through . . . Jesus Christ'.

So Romans 5:17 raises a challenge as we come to the end of this week. Are you 'reigning in life'? Of course, this will only be fully true in the life of the new creation. But here and now? Reflect in prayer on the extent to which your faith in the cross and resurrection of Christ has:

- rescued you from the pessimistic futility of death;
- given you hope and comfort in times when life itself has become 'deathly';
- filled you with joyful anticipation of that feast with God when death itself will be swallowed up;
- taken away all fear of death itself, although, truth be told, we still recoil from dying;
- inspired you to resist the reign of sin, and count yourself alive to God in Christ; Jesus (6:11–14): 'For sin shall no longer be your master.'

Week 3
SINNERS FORGIVEN

Sunday
Forgiveness full and free

If you, LORD, kept a record of sins,
    Lord, who could stand?
But with you there is forgiveness,
    Therefore you are to be feared.
(Psalm 130:3–4)

Blessed is the one
    whose transgressions are forgiven,
    whose sins are covered.
Blessed is the one
    whose sin the LORD does not count against them
    and in whose spirit is no deceit.
When I kept silent,
    my bones wasted away
    through my groaning all day long.
For day and night
    your hand was heavy on me;
my strength was sapped
    as in the heat of summer.
Then I acknowledged my sin to you
    and did not cover up my iniquity.
I said, 'I will confess
    my transgressions to the LORD.'
And you forgave
    the guilt of my sin.
(Psalm 32:1–5)

The loud shout of victory is the single word *tetelestai*. Being in the perfect tense, it means 'it has been and will forever remain finished'.

We note the achievement Jesus claimed just before he died. It is not men who have finished their brutal deed; it is he who has accomplished what he came into the world to do. He has borne the sins of the world. Deliberately, freely and in perfect love he has endured the judgment in our place. He has procured salvation for us, established a new covenant between God and humankind, and made available the chief covenant blessing, the forgiveness of sins.

In conclusion, the cross enforces three truths – about ourselves, about God and about Jesus Christ.

First, our sin must be extremely horrible. Nothing reveals the gravity of sin like the cross. For ultimately what sent Christ there was neither the greed of Judas, nor the envy of the priests, nor the vacillating cowardice of Pilate, but our own greed, envy, cowardice and other sins, and Christ's resolve in love and mercy to bear judgment and so put them away. It is impossible for us to face Christ's cross with integrity and not to feel ashamed of ourselves. Apathy, selfishness and complacency blossom everywhere in the world except at the cross. There these noxious weeds shrivel and die. They are seen for the tatty, poisonous things they are. For if there was no way by which the righteous God could righteously forgive our unrighteousness, except that he should bear it himself in Christ, it must be serious indeed. It is only when we see this that, stripped of our self-righteousness and self-satisfaction, we are ready to put our trust in Jesus Christ as the Saviour we urgently need.

Secondly, God's love must be wonderful beyond comprehension. God could quite justly have abandoned us to our fate. He could have left us alone to reap the fruit of our wrongdoing and to perish in our sins. It is what we deserved. But he did not. Because he loved us, he came after us in Christ. He pursued us even to the desolate anguish of the cross, where he bore our sin, guilt, judgment and death. It takes a hard and stony heart to remain unmoved by love like that. It is more than love. Its proper name is 'grace', which is love to the undeserving.

Thirdly, Christ's salvation must be a free gift. He 'purchased' it for us at the high price of his own life-blood. So what is there left for us to pay? Nothing! Since he claimed that all was now 'finished', there is nothing for us to contribute. Not of course that we now have licence to sin and can always count on God's forgiveness. On the contrary, the same cross of Christ, which is the ground of a free salvation, is also the most powerful incentive to a holy life. But this new life follows. First, we have to humble ourselves at the foot of the cross, confess that we have sinned and deserve nothing at his hand but judgment, thank him that he loved us and died for us, and receive from him a full and free forgiveness.

John Stott, *The Cross of Christ*, pp. 97–99

Monday
'What a great sin'

Bible reading: Exodus 32:1–14

A brutal shock

If you'd been reading the book of Exodus up to this point, at 32:1–6 you'd feel that the story crashes to earth right here. Here are people who have experienced God's greatest act of redemption in human history (chapters 1–18) – until the crucifixion and resurrection of Christ will take place. Here are people who, in the midst of earth-shaking events at Mount Sinai, have received from God their identity and mission to be God's priestly and holy people among all the nations in the whole earth (19:3–6). Here are people who have received God's gifts of grace for a redeemed community – God's law and covenant, to which they have responded by promising three times to obey all that God commanded (chapters 20–24). Here are people in whose midst the living God wants to dwell, and to whom he has given detailed instructions for the tent in which he will do so (chapters 25–31).

In these last seven chapters, you'll have been in the glorious presence of God with Moses on the mountaintop, just trying to visualize the sumptuous beauty, the intricacies of white, blue and scarlet embroidery, the glinting of gold and silver and bronze, the warm glow of oil lamps and the fragrance of incense – all to adorn the place where God wished to dwell.

The fall of Israel

But in six verses of blatant disobedience and idolatry with a ridiculous calf made of melted gold earrings, Aaron and the people break the first three of the Ten Commandments. They explicitly reject the God who had brought them up out of Egypt (20:2–3; 32:4). They make an idol. And they abuse the name of Yahweh in a blasphemous parody of the covenant ceremony (32:5–6; 24:5, 11). It's like committing adultery on your wedding night. It's like the story of the fall in Genesis 3, after the beauty of Genesis 1 – 2. This is the fall of Israel.

For here also are the people whom God has created and called to be the means of blessing to the nations (Genesis 12:1–3). But Israel turns out to be just as sinful as the rest of humanity: rebellious, idolatrous, immoral. The people through whom God wills to bring healing to the nations are themselves infected by the virus of sin and rebellion. We should be shocked and depressed.

What can God do? Well, he could wipe out this bunch of stiff-necked rebels and start again with Moses instead of Abraham (verse 10). But in the very act of suggesting that and warning Moses to stand aside, God mysteriously *pauses* for a moment (after all, God could have just acted without telling Moses at all, couldn't he?). God leaves space for grace, the grace of intercession. It almost seems, don't you think, that God *wants* Moses to speak up. And he does. Fast.

Urgent intercession

Moses steps into the gap and boldly argues with God, objecting vigorously to the whole idea that God could utterly destroy this people (32:11–13). His intercession is split over two days, and today we see the first vital part – the beginnings of forgiveness. Moses makes three rapid but profound appeals.

1 *God's relationship with Israel (verse 11).* Look at verse 7, where God talked to Moses about 'your people whom you brought up out of Egypt'. But Moses robustly objects. 'Excuse me, Lord,' he says, 'but they are *your* people, and *you* brought them out of Egypt. They belong to you by your own redemption.' It is God who started this whole covenant relationship.

2 *God's name and reputation (verse 12).* What will the Egyptians think of Yahweh God if he takes so much trouble getting his

people out of slavery and then kills them anyway? What kind of malicious or incompetent god is that? Think again, God!

3 *God's covenant promise (verse 13).* 'Remember ... Abraham.' God could not go back on the oath he had sworn on his own life. In appealing to God to change his mind at this terrifying moment, Moses was actually appealing to God to be consistent with his ancient promise and all it would mean for Israel – and indeed for the world.

Moses's words go straight to the heart of what matters most to God: his redeeming *love*, his *name* and his covenant *promise*. And, on those grounds, God withholds his threatened destruction.

The same three things should still be the foundation for our own intercessory prayers – during Lent and always. Why not think what they mean for you, with some other appropriate scriptures that emphasize the same assurance for our prayers? On what grounds do you make your requests to God?

Tuesday
'Forgive our wickedness and our sin'

Bible reading: Exodus 32:30 – 33:6; 33:12 – 34:9

'Why doesn't God just forgive us?'

Have you ever heard that said?

These chapters in Exodus expose the sheer depth of ungrateful rebellious depravity in human sin. And although we hear, with Moses, God's own resounding affirmation of his forgiving character (34:6–7), we also know, with Israel, that God cannot '*just forgive*'. Indeed, as we agonize through the suspense of the 'negotiation' between Moses and God (is that a fair word for these verses? It certainly sounds like it), we sense that forgiveness is a deep problem for God himself, a problem that only he can and ultimately will resolve. Forgiveness is not something casually dished out on demand, like sweets to a child.

Yesterday, the Lord had simply relented (32:14). Today, Moses specifically asks God to forgive – that is (in Hebrew), '*to carry*' – their 'great sin' (32:32). Somebody has to bear this sin. If the people do, it spells destruction. But if God will carry it himself, then they can be spared. That's the meaning of forgiveness: the offended party carrying the offence rather than inflicting its consequences on the offender.

'But if not . . .'

Most likely, Moses means that if God intended *not* to forgive (and so intended to destroy) the people, then he (Moses) has no wish to

68

carry on. Not so much offering to die *for* the people, as asking to perish *with* them, if that's what was to happen. Moses intercedes in a way that identifies himself completely with those he is praying for. Do our prayers ever reach that kind of depth?

God gives an enigmatic answer, which goes part way. He will keep one element of the promise to Abraham. Let Moses lead the people up into the land, with an angel to help. But God himself will not be in their midst – for their own protection (33:1–3). This is catastrophic! Without the presence of God in their midst, Israel would lose all their distinctiveness among the nations. That distinctiveness included the presence of God and holiness of life (Deuteronomy 4:5–8). All of that is now threatened. This won't do, will it? You might as well cancel chapters 25 – 31. No tabernacle, no ark of the covenant, no atoning sacrifices, no priests, no holy God dwelling in the Most Holy Place. A bleak prospect, if you'd been an Israelite. No wonder they stripped off their ornaments in repentant grief.

Moses wrestles on until God promises unambiguously that his presence will go with his people (33:12–17). Not just an angel up at the front, but God himself at the centre. They will travel together: God, Moses and the people. (Did you notice again in verse 16 how inseparably Moses unites himself with the people he prays for?)

Forgiven sinners are sinful still, however; they are 'stiff-necked' indeed, as Moses acknowledges in 34:9. That's why he asks God to go on carrying/forgiving them. God will have a lot more 'carrying' to do before this story is over. God must either bear our sin himself, or destroy us. And we will praise God for eternity that he chose the former.

Glory and goodness

But Moses hasn't finished yet. 'Now show me your *glory*,' he asks (verse 18). Wouldn't you think he would have had enough of the glory of God up that mountain for the past month? But Moses wants an even more intimate understanding of his God. God says he will cause all his *goodness* to pass in front of Moses. God's glory is his goodness. Or God's goodness is his glory. Either way: hallelujah!

This good and glorious God then defines himself in classic words that echo through Scripture:[1]

> the compassionate and gracious God, slow to anger, abounding in love and faithfulness, maintaining love to thousands, and forgiving *[carrying]* wickedness, rebellion and sin. Yet he does not leave the guilty unpunished . . .
> (34:6–7)

Let your mind dwell in prayer on the paradox of God and the mystery of forgiveness. Here is the God who 'carries' sin. But here also is the God who punishes the wicked.

How can this tension be resolved? Only finally at the cross, where God in Christ simultaneously did both. For indeed, God finally did *not* leave the guilty unpunished. But that was because God chose to bear the consequences of sin and guilt in his own self, in God's own Son.

---

1 If you want to hear those echoes, spend some time browsing through the following: Numbers 14:18; Nehemiah 9:17; Psalms 78:38; 86:5, 15; 99:8; 103:8; 145:8–9; Joel 2:13; Jonah 4:2; Micah 7:18–19.

Wednesday
'Ransomed, healed, restored, forgiven'

Bible reading: Psalm 103

Anger and forgiveness

Yesterday we saw God punishing sinners in his anger, but also forgiving sinners in his mercy. And we know from our New Testament that only the cross resolves this tension. But how did Old Testament Israelites hold these two aspects of God together? Did they imagine their God as permanently angry (the caricature 'God of the Old Testament')? Or did they think that God's forgiveness was a kind of weakness – that he just caved in to Moses' persistent request? Psalm 103 shows that the answer to both is no.

On the one hand, God's *anger* is utterly real and justified (Exodus 32:7–10), *but* limited. He is 'slow to anger' (Psalm 103: 8–9), and it does not last for ever, unlike his covenant love which will (verse 17). And, on the other hand, God's *forgiveness* defines not only his character (verse 8), but also his universal kingdom (verse 19). God forgives not with reluctance, but as the exercise of his everlasting power. Since he is the ruler of the universe (did you notice this point at the end of Psalm 103?), he has the strength to 'carry' a nation's sin (see Numbers 14:17–20).

He can carry your sin and mine, then. Personal forgiveness flows from God's throne.

Can you see how the author of Psalm 103 turns the Exodus story into his own personal testimony? God's acts of righteousness and justice for the oppressed (verse 6) were modelled in the exodus itself, as Moses and Israel knew well (verse 7). The psalmist urges his own soul, just as Moses urged Israel, not to forget all that God had done (Deuteronomy 6:12, 8:11). God's 'benefits' for him, as for Israel, included forgiveness (Exodus 34:9), healing[1] (Exodus 15:26) and redemption from the pit of utter destruction (Exodus 32:10, 14).

Feeling the heartbeat

Sometimes it helps us to get at the central message of a psalm if we take note of its structure. This one is beautifully balanced. We can recognize this by the way the writer repeats, in the second half of the psalm, certain key words or concepts in reverse order from the first half. Look for the repeated words in italics and notice how they occur in both halves of the Psalm.

Having begun with personal *praise* (verses 1–2), he ends by summoning *praise* from angels, cosmic powers and the whole created order, ending, as he began, with himself (verses 20–22). This is like an outer 'envelope' around the psalm. And then, within that outer circle (**A**), there are several inner concentric circles pointing inwards to the central heartbeat of the whole poem:

(**B**) The saving *righteousness* of God that had rescued exodus Israel (verse 6) is the same everlasting love and *righteousness* that will sustain those who love and fear the Lord in every generation (verses 17–18).

(**C**) The *Moses* of verse 7 is recalled in verses 14–16, where the dust and grass of human mortality echo the *Psalm of Moses* (Psalm 90:1–6). However, Psalm 103 links the theme to God's fatherly compassion, whereas Psalm 90 links it to God's wrath. Both perspectives, of course, are true and complementary.

(**D**) The *compassion* of God is first quoted directly from Exodus 34:6 (verse 8), and then quickly returns, compared to the *compassion* of a father (verse 13).

---

1 This is poetry. The psalmist knew that he, along with all humans, would one day succumb to mortal illness and die (verses 15–16). Psalm 103:3(b) is not a guarantee of healing from every illness, but a recognition that all healing of illness (present or ultimate) comes from the Lord.

And so we zoom in through these decreasing rings of matching words and phrases to the very centre of the psalm. And what is this core message, this beating heart of divine truth? Can you see it in all its heart-warming assurance in verses 9–12?

Read those wonderful words aloud with thankfulness in your heart!

> He will not always accuse,
>   nor will he harbour his anger for ever;
> he does not treat us as our sins deserve
>   or repay us according to our iniquities.
> For as high as the heavens are above the earth,
>   so great is his love for those who fear him;
> as far as the east is from the west,
>   so far has he removed our transgressions from us.

We can rejoice in what the Israelites, as a nation, learned at Mount Sinai: that God 'does not treat us as our sins deserve, or repay us according to our iniquities' (verse 10). If that were not true, I would not be writing this book and you would not be reading it. He is the God whose love is as high as the heavens (verse 11), and whose forgiveness is as wide as the globe (verse 12). That is the very nature of his 'throne in heaven'; that is the way his kingdom rules (verse 19). And that is why the One who came announcing the arrival of the reign of God in words of forgiveness, and works of healing and redemption, gladly accepted the insult 'Friend of sinners'.

That makes him your friend and mine. 'Bless the Lord, O my soul!'

Thursday
'Your sins have been forgiven'

Bible reading: Luke 7:29–50

'Friend of sinners' indeed! It might sound nice to you, but to me as a Pharisee (Simon by name), no worse accusation could be made against a rabbi – if Jesus could even be called that. But I'd been to hear John the Baptist, and I'd listened to Jesus from the back of the crowd, and they had certainly challenged my thinking. So I invited Jesus along with some of my Pharisee friends for a meal at my house.

So there we are, reclining and enjoying my wife's food and just getting ready to spring some hard questions on Jesus, when . . . in walks this woman! Or rather, *that* woman. We all knew who she was and *what* she was in our village. She walks up behind where Jesus was reclining, and breaks into great heaving sobs, with her tears splashing on to his bare feet. Then (the shock!) she lets her hair down, as loose as she is herself, and kneels down and wipes his feet and kisses them. And then she snaps open the neck of a jar of perfume and pours it all over his feet – and the voluptuous sexy scent fills my pure house. And Jesus? He just smiles, turns slightly, pats her on the shoulder – as if he'd met her before. I mean, surely not?

Well, we're all frozen into silence. I'm so embarrassed and I'm thinking, 'Whatever they say, this man is *not* a prophet and I'll tell you why. First, if he were a prophet, he'd know what kind of woman this creature is, even if he's never met her. Second, if he knew, he wouldn't dare let her touch him like that – *she's a dirty sinner!*' I am about to announce this when Jesus looks over at me, as if to say, 'I can answer that for you, Simon', as if he'd read my thoughts. And he starts telling a story.

74

'There were these two men who owed money to a moneylender. One owed about this much,' and Jesus picks up a rather large melon in one hand. 'The other owed about this much,' and he picks up an olive in the other. 'But the moneylender was a kind man' (yeah, right), 'so he said, "I know you boys can't pay me back, so I forgive both of you your debts."' And I'm thinking, 'What has this got to do with the situation here?' Then Jesus goes on, 'Which one of the two do you think will love the moneylender more?'

See, that's the annoying thing about Jesus. You come with a bunch of questions to ask *him* and he asks *you* one single question, and you're stumped. I wanted to give a clever answer, but in the end, I just mumbled, 'I suppose the one who had the bigger debt forgiven.' 'Good answer!' says Jesus with a smile. Then he swivels round a bit to look at the woman, but he's still talking to me over his shoulder. 'Do you see this woman?' Well, of course I could *see* her! Right here, uninvited, *in my house* . . . 'Your house, yes,' says Jesus. 'When I came in, you gave me none of the customary tokens of welcome. But she has not stopped treating me like her honoured guest.'

This is totally unfair and out of order. Comparing *me*, Simon, with *her* – and her a sinner! A really big-time sinner, too . . . But Jesus interrupts my thoughts again. 'Yes, she is indeed. Her sins are many. But here's the thing. *Her sins have been forgiven.* That's the difference. And *that's why* she shows me such love and honour.' Then he turns back, and looks straight at me across the table: 'But I suppose,' he adds quietly, 'someone who thinks they have nothing to be forgiven for will not show much love.'

Was that true? Did I really think I had little or nothing to be forgiven for? I felt myself blushing. This woman might be the biggest sinner in the room, but was she the only sinner? I looked around at my guests. Their eyes were out on stalks; they'd never been so close to a woman like that . . . and her hair . . . and the perfume . . . 'There is more sin going on right here in my house today than in hers,' I found myself thinking.

Jesus had turned my question upside down. The point is not, 'Who is the biggest sinner?' but, 'Which of us knows that our sins have been forgiven?'

Then Jesus turns round fully to the woman, gently lifts up her face and speaks directly to her. 'They *have* been forgiven, you know – your sins, all of them, as I told you, remember? Trust me!' That broke the silence! All round the table, 'Who does he think he is? Forgiving sins? *Only God can do that!*' Well, yes indeed. But Jesus just insists to the woman, *'Your sins have been forgiven.* Do you believe me?' She nods a smile through her tears. *'Then your faith has saved you. Go in peace.'*

She stands up, and having crept in despised, she walks out with the dignity of the forgiven.

And my conscience-stricken heart is crying out, 'Jesus, what would I give to have you say those words to me!'

Friday
'He bore our sins'

Bible reading: 1 Peter 2:19–25

'Your sins are forgiven'

It's all very well to say the words, but how can it be true? Did Exodus not tell us, 'God does not leave the guilty unpunished' (Exodus 34:7)? Did God himself not say, 'I will not acquit the guilty' (Exodus 23:7)? How, then, is forgiveness possible?

Sin has consequences that have to be borne. Guilt cries out for justice to be done. Deliberate evil demands some kind of punishment. Wrongdoing needs to be put right in some way. If those are among our deepest human instincts, how can God's holiness hold lesser standards?

Yet Exodus also showed us God's compassion, while Psalm 103 rejoiced in God's reigning love and forgiveness. We must hold both holiness and love together, for they are *both* definitive of our God, and they are not in competition with each other.

> This vision of God's holy love will deliver us from caricatures of him. We must picture him neither as an indulgent God who compromises his holiness in order to spare and spoil us, nor as a harsh, vindictive God who suppresses his love in order to crush and destroy us. How then can God express his holiness without consuming us, and his love without condoning our sins?
>
> (John Stott, *The Cross of Christ*, p. 155)

Answer: by bearing the consequences of our sin himself. As we saw, Moses asked God to 'carry' (i.e. forgive) the sins of Israel, and God agreed to do so. What Moses could not have imagined then was the ultimate cost to God not only of bearing the sin of Israel, but of 'tak[ing] away the sin of the world'. He would find out, however, in the conversation on the Mount of Transfiguration, when Moses, Elijah and Jesus would speak of the 'exodus' that Jesus would 'bring to fulfilment at Jerusalem' (Luke 9:31) – that greater 'exodus' redemption accomplished when Jesus '[would bear] our sins in his body on the cross' (1 Peter 2:24).

Suffering for Christ and like Christ

Peter is talking here to Christian slaves of unbelieving masters. And he points out that if the slaves get beaten for some wrongdoing, there is nothing Christianly commendable about that. That's simple, if brutal, justice. You get what you deserve. But if you suffer *unjustly* while doing good, ah, *that* is pleasing to God. Why? Not because God takes sadistic pleasure in your suffering, but because such suffering is like Christ's.

But Peter cannot talk about the suffering and death of Christ *merely* as an *example* (though it certainly is that). Jesus did not die merely to model how somebody could endure injustice and cruelty without fighting back. No, he suffered '*for you*' (verse 21). And in those two words, Peter condenses a profound atonement theology that he then expands through several quotations from Isaiah 53. 'Christ cannot be an example of suffering for us to follow unless he is first of all the Saviour whose sufferings were endured on our behalf' (I. Howard Marshall, *1 Peter*, p. 91).

To say that Christ bore our sins means that he bore their consequences and guilt, doing so in our place, for us. But who is this Christ? This is the Lord God himself, incarnate. The One who told Moses that he would 'carry' sin is the One who now does exactly that in the person of the Son of God. God the just Judge submits to being the unjustly judged. And, in bearing his own sentence, God accomplishes ultimate justice, for himself and for us. Holy love poured out in saving fullness and atoning power – amazing and wonderful.

Peter's message is not for slaves only. 'To this you were called...' he says (verse 21), but the 'you' has become 'we' in verse 24. Christ's atonement thus becomes the pattern of life for us all. The word 'sins' is emphatically up front in both halves of verse 24. This is how we could read it.

- Our sins are what Christ bore in his body on the cross for our forgiveness.
- Sins are therefore what must be put away, as we live instead for righteousness.

Let us give thanks for the first, and strive to obey the second.

Saturday
'He is faithful and just'

Bible reading: 1 John 1:5 – 2:2

'So that we might die to sins . . .'

Remember this from yesterday (1 Peter 2:24)? But do we? Can we? It is wonderful to know that when I come to the cross as a repentant sinner, I receive God's gifts of forgiveness, justification, new birth and eternal life. But what about the rest of my life as a Christian? On the one hand, I am told that I should 'die to sin' and 'go and sin no more'. On the other hand, I slip and fall into sin all too easily. Isn't that your experience too? How are we to cope with this tension? John exposes two opposite dangers, and insists that the atoning death of Christ provides the ongoing answer to both.

Two opposite dangers

The danger of trivializing sin

In the community John was writing to, some were making boastful claims. They claimed to be in fellowship with God who is light, yet their actual behaviour ('walking in darkness') belied that claim (verse 6). Worse, they claimed to 'be without sin' (verses 8, 10). This probably does not mean they claimed to have reached a state of sinless perfection. Rather, *either* they were saying that any sins they might commit after becoming Christians 'didn't count' – they incurred no further guilt or condemnation (possibly using a text like Romans 8:1). So they felt they could now sin with happy abandon (in spite of Paul's strong rejection of that implication in Romans 6). *Or* they were simply denying that some dubious behaviour was actually 'sin' – they found ways to excuse or redefine it with other harmless words. Whenever we trifle with sin in such ways (and there are plenty more, we know), we deceive ourselves, make God a liar and reject the emphatic teaching of his Word. Don't do it!

John gives us the right response with two 'Ifs' and two almost identical promises. *'If* we walk in the light' (verse 7; which is to live with transparent honesty in the light of God's presence), and *'if* we confess our sins' (verse 9; as a reality, not a triviality), then not only do we remain within the true fellowship of believers, but we experience the *continuing* power of the cross. 'The blood of Jesus', as I'm sure you know, means the sacrificial death of Christ – as it does throughout the New Testament (e.g. Acts 20:28; Colossians 1:20; 1 Peter 1:18–19; Revelation 5:9). So John means that *all* of our sins, including those committed after conversion, are 'covered' by the atonement of the cross.

And here's another thing. Confession leads to *cleansing*. It is wonderful that God, in his covenant faithfulness and justice (verse 9; Deuteronomy 32:4), *forgives* our sin. But sin defiles and dirties us like sticky, clinging filth. Proverbs' question, 'Who can say, "I have kept my heart pure, I am clean and without sin"?' (Proverbs 20:9) generates the psalmist's prayer (Psalm 51:7), and receives God's promise (Jeremiah 33:8; Ezekiel 36:25). Have a glance at those texts, and then see how John turns that promise into an *ongoing* present experience: 'The blood of Jesus goes on cleansing us from all sin.' I have soaked in the warm soapy bath of that verse many, many times. Isn't it delicious to be *clean* again?

The danger of being terrified by sin

Does John fear that the wonderful truth of verse 9 might lead his readers to feel just a little too casual about sin? ('Well, I can always confess it and get forgiven again.') If so, he corrects such an inference immediately in 2:1. His whole purpose in writing is to strengthen them in resisting sin altogether – 'so that you will *not* sin'! Isn't that your longing, like every believer, going back to Psalm 119:9–11? 'But if anybody *does* sin . . .' – that is the reality for every believer too. What then? Do I stand condemned before God, tormented by Satan the accuser? No! says John. I stand amazed in the presence of Jesus my Advocate and Defender. His righteousness and atoning sacrifice (2:2) drive out the accuser, and will eternally destroy his works (1 John 3:8).

Think about why John uses exactly the same Greek word for Jesus (in 2:1 – 'Righteous One') as for God (in 1:9 – 'just'). This is the covenant righteousness of God that Old Testament saints appealed to for their salvation (e.g. Psalms 71:2, 15, 19–24; 85:9–11). And it is equally as true of Jesus as of the Father.

John's picture is not of a loving Jesus over against a just God, but of the just and righteous God, *both Father and Son together*, securing our eternal deliverance from guilt and condemnation. Let the end of this week of Lent fill you with the happy assurance of the continuing truth and power of the cross as affirmed in 1 John 1:8 – 2:2. I committed these verses to memory as a child, and I know I will never grow out of needing them.

Week 4

ENEMIES RECONCILED

Sunday
Blessed are the peacemakers

In the last days
the mountain of the Lord's temple will be established
   as the highest of the mountains;
it will be exalted above the hills,
   and peoples will stream to it.
Many nations will come and say,
'Come, let us go up to the mountain of the Lord,
   to the temple of the God of Jacob.
He will teach us his ways,
   so that we may walk in his paths.'
The law will go out from Zion,
   the word of the Lord from Jerusalem.
He will judge between many peoples
   and will settle disputes for strong nations far and wide.
They will beat their swords into ploughshares
   and their spears into pruning hooks.
Nation will not take up sword against nation,
   nor will they train for war any more.
Everyone will sit under their own vine
   and under their own fig tree,
and no one will make them afraid,
   for the Lord Almighty has spoken.
All the nations may walk
   in the name of their gods,
but we will walk in the name of the Lord
   our God for ever and ever.
(Micah 4:1–5)

The cross not only elicits our worship . . . but it also directs our conduct in relation to others, including our enemies . . . We are to exhibit in our relationships that combination of love and justice which characterized the wisdom of God in the cross.

But how, in practice, we are to combine love and justice, mercy and severity, and so walk in the way of the cross, is often hard to decide and harder still to do. Take 'conciliation' or 'peace-making' as an example. Christian people are called to be peacemakers (Mt. 5:9) and to 'seek peace and pursue it' (1 Pet. 3:11) . . . In pronouncing peacemakers 'blessed', Jesus added that 'they will be called sons (or daughters) of God'. He must have meant that peace-making is such a characteristically divine activity that those who engage in it thereby disclose their identity and demonstrate their authenticity as God's children.

If our peace-making is to be modelled on our heavenly Father's, however, we shall conclude at once that it is quite different from appeasement. For the peace which God secures is never cheap peace, but always costly. He is indeed the world's pre-eminent peacemaker, but when he determined on reconciliation with us, his 'enemies', who had rebelled against him, he 'made peace' through the blood of Christ's cross (Col. 1:20). To reconcile himself to us, and us to himself, and Jews, Gentiles and other hostile groups to one another, cost him nothing less than the painful shame of the cross. We have no right to expect, therefore, that we shall be able to engage in conciliation work at no cost to ourselves, whether our involvement in the dispute is as the offending or offended party, or as a third party anxious to help enemies to become friends again . . .

The incentive to peace-making is love, but it degenerates into appeasement whenever justice is ignored. To forgive and to ask for forgiveness are both costly exercises. All authentic Christian peace-making exhibits the love and justice – and so the pain – of the cross.

John Stott, *The Cross of Christ*, pp. 341–343

Monday
Brothers reconciled

Bible reading: Genesis 50:15–21

This is a beautiful *ending*, don't you think? This moment of brotherly reconciliation. Especially when you remember the jagged turbulence of the early chapters of Genesis following the beautiful *beginning* in chapters 1 – 2.

Broken relationships at every level saturate Genesis 3 – 11. Shame and domination poison marriage. Jealousy and anger lead to a brother's murder. Corruption and violence blight the whole human race. And nations are scattered in confusion. It's not just that every individual is a sinner. By the time we reach Genesis 11, sin has brought God's curse on the earth, pervaded culture, escalated through generations and divided the nations. How can such brokenness be healed, such enmities be reconciled?

So along comes God's answer in Genesis 12: Abraham and his family, through whom God is going to enable all nations to find blessing like his. But as we read the long chapters that follow, episodes of blessing seem like sporadic relief from the long catalogue of hatred and violence. Can you imagine any more dysfunctional family than Abraham's, through four generations? Squabbling wives, abused women, lying men, sibling rivalry, trickery and deception, sexual violence, slaughter, murderous hatred . . . on and on it goes.

The miracle of Genesis is that God keeps going too, repeating his promise to each generation: 'All nations *will* be blessed through you, trust me.' And so the book comes to this gentle conclusion that is movingly beautiful and theologically rich. This is what God truly longs for, it seems to say – reconciliation, healing, peace.

Mind you, it all begins very dubiously – more lies! Out of fear of vengeance (in spite of 45:4–11), Joseph's brothers invent their dead father's plea for Joseph to forgive the wrongs they had done. Twice they admit their sin; twice they ask for forgiveness. That's a start, I suppose.

Joseph's response is the message of the whole book in a nut-shell. Here are the radical truths on which reconciliation could be based – then, now or at any time.

- *The sovereignty of God* (verse 19). 'If you want forgiveness,' Joseph is saying, 'you need to take it up with a higher court. I may be top guy in Egypt, but I'm not God. Forgiveness is for God to dispense. So don't be afraid. I'm not the one to be afraid of here.'
- *The providence of God* (verse 20). No excuses. No 'You didn't really mean it, did you?' Just plain truth. '*You* planned evil against me.' Absolutely. But then comes the redemptive power of God to make evil accomplish *his* good plans: 'But *God* planned it for good.' And God's plan – overriding evil to accomplish good – resulted in the saving of lives.
- *The refusal of vengeance* (verse 21). So, if that was God's plan, how could Joseph reverse it back into the evil of an endless unforgiving feud between brothers? No, let God's plan stand. 'So, to repeat: don't be afraid, not only will I not take revenge, I will positively care for you and your children.'

Those last three words, 'and your children', were what convinced some Arabic-speaking tribesmen in Chad, when they first listened to the book of Genesis translated into their own language, that Joseph and his brothers were truly reconciled. The translators asked them how they could be sure. It was not so much Joseph's grand theology, but his promise to care for their children. 'That's what brothers do,' they exclaimed. 'Of course they are reconciled!'

Joseph's words and example point us to the cross. Can you see the same fundamental dynamic in the way Peter describes the cross in Acts 2:23–24? That too was planned as deliberate evil – the worst that human wickedness could hurl at the Son of God. But God in his sovereign providence and foreknowledge turned that evil to its own destruction, and brought about the infinite good of the saving of lives – eternally. Radical reconciliation is God's *good* triumphing over humankind's *evil*.

Are there circumstances in your life that might need the tough words of 1 Peter 2:19–25 and 4:12–16?

Peter fortifies us with the example of Jesus, but he could have pointed to Joseph too. And Paul insists also that reconciliation with enemies cannot come about through vengeance, but only by imitating God himself, who overcame evil with good (Romans 12:17–21). Pray for this to be your attitude and practice.

Tuesday
Nations reconciled

Bible reading: Isaiah 19:18–25

Do you sometimes wonder how the prophets got away with it? Without being lynched on the spot, I mean?

Take the last verse of Isaiah's prophecy here. He puts the arch-enemies of Israel on a par with Israel itself, and salutes them with God-given titles that the Israelites jealously guarded for themselves. Would you have stood for such blasphemous nonsense if you'd been an Israelite? Me neither. But I'm jumping ahead.

The first surprise in this passage is what comes immediately before it. Just look at Isaiah 19:1–17. It is a typical piece of prophetic denunciation, in God's name, of the whole nation of Egypt in Isaiah's own day. Egypt, like so many other nations, stands under God's judgment. But then, in a totally unexpected reversal, God makes promises of incredible blessing for Egypt – at some indefinite future ('in that day . . .'). 'Egypt' now seems to stand in a symbolic, collective sense for any and all nations that have been God's enemies, but will, in God's time and by God's power, undergo a radical transformation and reconciliation with God and with one another.

We marvel at this list of blessings.

- *The worship of God* (verses 18–19). Egypt will want so much to show their new-found faith in Yahweh the God of Israel that they will learn Israel's language and worship Yahweh instead of Ra, the great sun god of Egypt, in his city, Heliopolis. Like Abraham, they will build an altar to the Lord in their own land.

- *The salvation of God* (verse 20). From Genesis to Exodus. When the Egyptians themselves do what the Hebrews did in Egypt – cry out to the Lord out of oppression – he will send them a Moses of their own to save and deliver them. This is Exodus reloaded. And who might that 'Saviour' be?
- *The knowledge of God* (verse 21). The Pharaoh refused to 'know the Lord' – that is, to acknowledge that Yahweh was God – and refused to let the Hebrews go out and worship him (Exodus 5:1–2). But now they *will* acknowledge the Lord and worship him themselves.
- *The healing of God* (verse 22). Plagues! We know all about them, all ten of them (Exodus 7 – 12). But when those who suffer God's blows turn to him in repentance and pleading, God will respond in mercy and healing. The healer of Israel becomes the healer of Israel's enemies (Exodus 15:26)!
- *The blessing of God* (verses 23–24). As if Egypt were not enough, Isaiah adds Assyria. Now those two empires of the west and the east were like giant nutcrackers, periodically crushing little Israel between them over the centuries. And now they will come together – not to attack Israel as before, but to join Israel in worship. *And* (most surprising of all), to share Israel's Abrahamic mission of being 'a blessing on the earth'. Those blessed with God's radical reconciliation become agents of blessing and reconciliation themselves – a thought that would also occur to Paul.
- *The people of God* (verse 25). And so to the climax. Isaiah takes three phrases that were the unparalleled privilege of Israel: to be called by God 'my people', 'my handiwork', and 'my inheritance'. He spreads them out across all three nations. The word order in Hebrew is 'Blessed be my people, *Egypt* (!), and my handiwork, *Assyria* (!), and my inheritance, *Israel* (!)'. God has made the three one, co-sharers in the blessing of being his own people. He has reconciled those who were enemies of God and enemies of one another.

This astonishing prophecy is just one of many passages in the Old Testament that envisage the one living God of Israel bringing the nations to know and worship him, in blessing and peace (like the one we read on Sunday).[1] It was this scriptural vision that fired the Gentile mission of the early church. God was in the business of making his enemies his friends (as the Apostle Paul knew more than most). He still is.

> [The LORD] makes wars cease
>   to the ends of the earth.
> He breaks the bow and shatters the spear;
>   he burns the shields with fire.
> He says, 'Be still, and know that I am God;
>   I will be exalted among the nations,
>   I will be exalted in the earth.'
> (Psalm 46:9–10)

Give thanks today for the reconciling power of the gospel. For Hutu and Tutsi Christian students during the Rwandan genocide who were told to separate, but held hands in prayer, saying, 'We have lived together; we will die together.' For Korean and Japanese students I knew at All Nations Christian College, UK, who could love and embrace one another in spite of their nations' histories. For Palestinian Christians and Messianic Jews I know who share their pain together and struggle for reconciliation between their communities. Only the Radical Reconciler can do such things.

Pray today for Christians living in conflict zones and working for justice, peace and reconciliation.

---

1 Others include: 1 Kings 8:41–43; Psalms 22:27; 67; 86:8–10; 87; Isaiah 45:22–24; 56:3–8; Amos 9:11–12; Zechariah 2:11.

Wednesday
A son reconciled

Bible reading: Luke 15:11–32

Well, OK, I know I'm only a fictional character. But Jesus is real, and the people listening to the story I'm in were real. Did you notice them, in Luke 15:1–2, the religious people who disapproved of the kind of people – 'the sinners' – that Jesus was welcoming? Didn't he know what fate awaited such people – and him too, if he was so friendly with them? That's who Jesus was challenging.

So Jesus invented me. A father. I'm sure he was thinking of his own Father as well.

Let me tell you about myself. I'm blessed with a good farm, sheep and cattle and a large house at the top of the village; I'm the biggest landowner, a senior citizen, well respected. And I've got these two sons. So, of course, they will inherit all my land when I die – a great future for them (though a long way off, I hope!).

But one day – I could hardly believe it! – my younger son comes and says, 'OK, Father, I want my share of the inheritance. Not some time in the future. Right here and now. Sign here, please.'

Unheard of. There is no provision in our law for a son to get his inheritance before his father dies. It was as if he couldn't wait for me to die. My own son actually wishing me dead! It was like a knife in my heart. For I knew what he really wanted was to take it and leave – go his own way, grab his freedom and forget all about me.

I think Jesus was making me feel the way his own Father must have felt when you, real people, chose to take everything God has given you, and then walk away from him and live as if he didn't exist. You chose to live in God's world as if God were dead. How do you think that makes God feel?

What should I have done? The whole village (who found out quickly) expected me to give the lad a thrashing, refuse his demand and probably cut him off completely. Wanting me dead, indeed!

But I didn't. I loved that boy. I did what he asked and gave him his freedom. So he sold his portion of land (*my* land!) as fast as he could, took the money and left home and the village in total disgrace. In fact, I heard he left the country, for a foreign unclean land of Gentiles – even more shame. As far as our family was concerned, he was as good as dead.

The news I heard of him through my travelling business friends was mixed. For a while he was having a great time – lots of friends, parties galore – except he was spending what really belonged to me, but without a thought for me in his head. But then famine came, food ran out, money ran out and he ended up starving on a pig farm. My son! Begging like a slave with filthy animals in an unclean land! It broke my heart. I wept. I loved that boy.

But it pleased the villagers! 'Serves the son right,' they were saying. 'He's got what he deserved for the way he treated his father. That's what happens, see, to sinners like him. And just right too.' And then I realized ... those real people listening to Jesus would agree with the villagers. 'Good story, Jesus,' they would think. 'We agree with you. God will make sure that sinners get what they deserve in the end, just like that shameful son. Let him rot in pig filth like himself! That's the right ending, Jesus.' And they were turning away, nodding, satisfied that Jesus wasn't as soft on sinners as they had thought.

Except it wasn't the end of Jesus' story. Or mine. Early every morning I used to go to the flat rooftop of my house where I could see across the village to the countryside beyond, hoping to catch sight of my son if ever he might try to creep back. And, one day, there he was, my own son! Ragged, barefoot and staggering, but I'd have known him a mile off. But his timing was all wrong. The village was already up and about as he drew near. I knew what would happen if he got into the street: he would face pent-up condemnation and rejection. They would spit and throw stones, maybe set the dogs on him, certainly throw him out as a disgrace. Only one person in the whole village could save him from that.

So I ran, *I ran!* Now, you need to understand, respected old men like me can't be seen hitching up our robes and exposing our legs in public. *We do not run.* But I did that day. With my servants trying to keep up, I ran down that street. Dogs were barking. Street kids were laughing and pointing. People were horrified. It was humiliating and shameful. But I had to put myself in the place where my son would be if I didn't get to him first. All this abuse and shame would be his – should be his. He was the one who deserved it. But I took it – humbling myself to spare him humiliation. (Did I tell you I loved that boy?)

I reached him at last. He had stopped, amazed, and began to sag as if he would kiss my feet. But I threw my arms around him (how he stank!), held him up and kissed *his face. I kissed him!* My runaway son. My disgrace of a son. Right there, in front of the whole village (who had tumbled out of the street behind me), I did the very opposite of what they expected. They could not believe that I still loved him and would *honour* him with a kiss, after the dishonour he had brought on us all.

He began a little speech about having sinned (true enough), but I interrupted him and called out loudly to my servants. 'Get my best robe, the ornamental one I wear on special occasions, and put it over these rags. And fetch the signet ring of our family and put it on his finger. And for goodness' sake bring some sandals. Only slaves and children go barefoot. *My son* will not walk into town with bare feet.' With those three things, I gave him back his dignity, his identity and his self-respect. I gave him back his life, really.

Then I announced even more loudly to the whole crowd, 'Tonight we will have a party at my house. You must accept what I do here. Honour me by coming to celebrate. For, yes, *this is my son* [they had expected me to disown him]. He was dead [he was, indeed, dead to me, to the family – and to himself]. But I have given him back his life. He was lost, but I have restored him. *I have reconciled him to myself* – and therefore to you, for my sake.' And then I walked with my arm around him, father and son reconciled, back up the street, back through the village, back to our home – his home.

I could feel Jesus looking through my eyes directly at those religious people. It's as if he were saying to them,

'If my Father and I choose to show costly love and compassion to the people you despise – the outcasts, the lowlife, the sinners; if we choose to suffer humiliation for their sake, to restore them and give them their lives back; if we choose to treat them as children of God, then you ought to be celebrating with us, not complaining and condemning. But if you will not be reconciled with those whom I have reconciled to God, then you will cut yourselves off from my Father and miss the greatest party ever known.
Your choice.'

But that's another part of my story.

Thursday
Jews and Gentiles reconciled

Bible reading: Ephesians 2:11–22

Were you ever left out as a child? Not picked for the team? Not invited to the party? It really hurt, didn't it, to feel excluded?

How much more so, then, for the truly excluded and marginalized of today's world. War and famine refugees, the homeless and landless. And these physical tragedies reflect the even greater spiritual plight of vast numbers alienated from God, needing to be brought home – home to peace with God and one another.

Our passage today has to be the most classic, exalted reconciliation text in the Bible, wouldn't you agree? It is simply bursting with the good news of what the Radical Reconciler has accomplished, and the cross is at its very heart. It's a bit dense, so let's unravel its three stages.

Three stages
Then and now (verses 11–13)
When Paul says 'You', he means his Gentile readers, disparagingly lumped together by Jews as 'the uncircumcision'. That was the greatest chasm in Paul's world – the hostility between Jews and Gentiles. Paul reminds those citizens of Ephesus of what they had been before they came to faith in Christ. Every phrase of verse 12 is a blighting negative, a catalogue of deprivation and alienation. Without any knowledge of the Scriptures, the Gentiles had been separated from Israel's Messiah, Israel's community, Israel's promise, Israel's hope and Israel's God. Wealthy, sophisticated, cultured citizens of a great imperial city they may have been. But this was the spiritual truth about them – as is still true not only for

those who lived before Christ, but for all who live without Christ. It was true of us all once. Far from the living God, far from home.

'*But now!*' Verse 13 is a staggering transformation. In Christ and through his blood, the distant have been brought near, the separated have been connected, the outsiders have been brought in, the alienated have been reconciled. The gospel brings us home! The hurts can be healed. How could we not be excited by verse 13?

How and why (verses 14–18)

Paul's explanation of how the cross has accomplished such amazing reconciliation focuses on the word 'peace'. It comes three times.

- Christ *is* our peace (verse 14). Peace is Jesus-shaped. It is not a process or a state or an ideal. Peace is a personal relationship with Christ, shared by both parties.
- Christ *made* peace (verses 15–16). And he did this in three steps.
  (i) *He dissolved the barrier that divided Jews from Gentiles.* Paul means the law – not as the good and gracious gift of God, as he calls it in Romans 7, but as the barrier that had shut the Gentiles out and the Jews in, as a kind of badge of exclusive identity and privilege. The law in that sense, a barrier of pride and prejudice, was abolished on the cross.
  (ii) *He united the two in one new humanity.* It was not that Gentiles had to become Jews, but that Jews and Gentiles together become a whole new reality – a new kind of humanity in Christ. This is horizontal reconciliation. One plus one no longer makes two – but a new 'one'!
  (iii) *He reconciled both together in one body (i.e. the church) to God.* This is vertical reconciliation. Those who are brought together *as one* through the cross are brought together *to God* through the cross. Paul insists that you can't have one without the other. Both are central to the gospel. Jews and Gentiles in Christ are no longer enemies; that's because God, rather than slaying his enemies, has slain the enmity itself at the cross (verse 16). That is radical reconciliation. It deals with the roots.

- Christ came and *preached* peace (verses 17–18). When? Jesus never went to Ephesus! No, but when the *apostles* preached the gospel of reconciliation, Jesus himself was proclaiming the peace that he achieved on the cross, to people far and near (Paul has Isaiah 57:7 and 19 in mind) – Gentiles and Jews.

So what? (verses 19–22)

Paul's magnificent climax assures the Ephesians ('You' still means those once far-off Gentiles) that their status is completely changed. Like Israel of the Old Testament, they have become citizens of *God's country*, members of *God's family* and the place of *God's dwelling*. What a transformation! From being in a place where God was absent, they have become the place where God himself has taken up residence.

And *you* and I are included in Paul's 'You'.

Dwell on the wonderful sequence of changes God has brought about for us. In verse 13, we get to come *near* to God. By verse 18, we get to come right into the Father's *presence*. By verse 22, we get to have God come and live within us, as his *temple*, God's address on earth.

What a privilege that we should be allowed to live in God's home. But how much more wonderful that God should make his home in us.

Friday
Accept one another

Bible reading: Romans 14:13 – 15:13

Paul had a problem. God had blessed his long years of missionary church-planting in Asia Minor and Greece (15:18–19). Now he believed God was calling him to head further west, to Spain, after taking his collection of money from the Gentile churches to the Jewish believers in Jerusalem. And he wanted to make the church in Rome his sending base for that new phase of his gospel mission, just as the church in Antioch had served for his mission in the eastern regions (15:23–29).

So what was his problem?

Condemnation and contempt

It appears that there were tensions among the believers in Rome, possibly between different house groups that met in the city. There were divisions over whether or not Christians should observe Jewish customs from the Torah regarding food and Sabbaths (14:2, 5). Some thought those rules were still mandatory and *condemned* those who ignored them. Others thought such rules were irrelevant and were *contemptuous* of those who still observed them. 'We're strong Christians, not weaklings like you with all your scruples!' There would have been Gentile and Jewish believers in both camps. Paul had heard about it. And it seriously threatened his plans. Why?

Undermining gospel mission

Think about it. How could Paul go to Spain preaching the gospel of reconciliation (horizontal and vertical, as we saw yesterday), if his sending church was a visible denial of it? His message would be completely undermined if these very people who had sent him were living in unreconciled conflict. If the news of those tensions had already reached Paul, it would certainly reach Spain. News from Rome travelled far and fast. Disunity in the church was a serious matter for Paul (as you can tell from his other letters too). It threatened the integrity of his mission. And it threw into question the truth of the gospel. *That is serious.*

So, can you see why Paul argues and appeals so passionately and at such length in this closing section of his letter (14–15)? This is not just, 'Please try to be a little nicer to one another, if you don't mind my asking.' This is a crucial matter that affects Paul's whole calling and mission from God to the world (15:15–16).

In the light of that, fill in, in your own mind, all the reasons Paul gives for his basic appeal, that Christians, in the midst of such 'disputable matters' (14:1; Paul does not deny that such things exist between believers), should *'accept one another'* (or *welcome*; it's a warm, embracing word). The fundamental command begins and ends his exhortation (14:1; 15:7).

Here are his major reasons.

- *Life before the Lord* (14:5–10). Who are you living for? Paul writes the word 'the Lord' seven times in these verses – the crucified and risen Lord (verse 9). He is the one before whom we live now, and to whom we shall give account. Will these differences matter then? If so, don't let them divide you now.
- *The demands of love* (14:15). 'No longer acting in love' – a terribly serious indictment for any Christian, given Christ's repeated commandment. And, even worse, to behave thus towards 'someone for whom Christ died' – as he did for you.
- *The hard work of peace* (14:17–19; 15:13). Nobody pretends it is easy. We have to 'make every effort' to do what is constructive and peace-building. For it is the work of the kingdom of God, the service of Christ, and pleasing to God.
- *The example of Christ* (15:3–7). The supreme reason is one Paul leaves until last (and it blends into the next one). How can one

Christian say to another, 'Christ may have welcomed you, but I don't'? That is the stance of the elder brother in Jesus' story – a dangerous, self-excluding hardness of heart. It's far from the 'one mind and one voice' that should adorn our worship if we truly make Christ's attitude our own.

- *The mission of God* (15:8–12). These verses are the climax of Paul's whole letter. His message has been that through the death and resurrection of the Messiah, God's Servant, the God of Israel has proved his righteousness by keeping his promise to Abraham. He has brought the Gentiles into the blessing of salvation along with Jews who put their faith in Messiah Jesus, and, as the Scriptures foretold, they will praise the God of David together. In the light of God's biblical mission to all nations and your share in it, *accept one another, just as Christ accepted you, in order to bring praise to God.*

Do you belong to a Christian community where there is disunity, 'quarrelling over disputable matters'? Why not encourage your sisters and brothers to give some time to a serious study of Romans 14 – 15 before making any further attempts to tackle the issues you face?

Saturday
Love one another

Bible reading: 1 John 3:11–23; 4:7–21

It seems right to end this week's reflections on the reconciling power of God, supremely demonstrated at the cross, with these deeply challenging words of John about love.

Wouldn't you agree that love – radically reconciling and healing love – has been at work in all our readings? Reconciling brothers, turning enemies into worshippers, restoring a disgraced son, dissolving the barrier between Jew and Gentile, surmounting 'disputable matters' with Christlike mutual acceptance.

So why is this matter of loving one another within the reconciled fellowship of forgiven sinners so critically important? John gives enormous space to it in his letter, just as he recorded Jesus stressing it repeatedly in his Gospel (John 13:34–35; 15:9–17). In fact, he bookends the whole section we have read with love as a *commandment*, not an option (3:11; 4:21).

Ponder at least four reasons that John gives.

Love is evidence of life (3:14–15)

Verse 14 echoes Jesus' words, 'Very truly I tell you, whoever hears my word and believes him who sent me has eternal life and will not be judged, but has crossed over from death to life' (John 5:24). John adds here that love is the proof that this has happened. From a world characterized by death since the very first murder by Cain, we are instead to give evidence of the eternal life within us through mutual love.

Love is evidence of Christ (3:16–18)

It is Christ who has shown us what love truly is, through giving his life for us in atoning sacrifice. (John repeats the point in 4:9–10). The cross, then, has to be the model for our own self-sacrificing love for one another. For just as neither God nor Jesus merely *said* that they loved us but proved it with action, so must we, in the most basic and practical ways.

Love is evidence of faith (3:23)

Another major theme in this letter is that *obedience* to God's commands is an essential mark of a truly born-again believer. In this respect, John and James are at one. Faith without the evidence of deeds is not faith at all – it's just dead (James 2:14–26). But what is God's primary command? Did you spot that in verse 23? John says, 'This is his *command*' – singular! Just *one* fundamental command. But he then defines that singular command as *two* things: to believe in Christ *and* 'to love one another as he commanded us'. These two are one; they cannot be separated. You cannot claim to be doing the first (trusting Christ) if you are not doing the second. Paul would have called this 'the obedience of faith' (Romans 1:5; 16:26).

Love is evidence for God (4:7–12)

John means this in two ways, and the second is astonishing. First, all true love flows from God himself for, in John's famous words, 'God is love' (4:16). So not to love is not to know God at all.

But, second, Christian love makes God visible! 'No one has ever seen God.' Where have you heard those words before? John put exactly those words at the beginning of his Gospel (John 1:18). Through the incarnation of the Word made flesh in Jesus, God 'solved the problem of his own invisibility' (as John Stott used to say). 'Anyone who has seen me has seen the Father,' Jesus later said (John 14:9). That was all very fine for those who did actually meet Jesus on earth. What about the rest of us? What about the rest of the world? Ah, says John, that's where we come in. If we demonstrate the powerful reconciling love of God among ourselves, 'God lives in us.' God makes himself visible in Christians who love one another!

That raises the searching question: when people look at us Christians, what do they see? The God of sacrificial love? The Radical Reconciler himself?

Ponder with me also the sobering negative implications of all John's points here. Where Christians do not live in reconciled love for one another, they raise questions over whether they have truly passed from death to life, they trample on the example of Christ and his cross, they disobey Christ's command and negate their faith, they can scarcely claim to know God and (perhaps worst of all) they make God invisible to the world around them. And, having pondered, spend some time in prayer for your own church and other churches to be delivered from such a danger.

Week 5

HISTORY GOVERNED

Sunday
The ruler of creation and history

Do you not know?
> Have you not heard?

Has it not been told you from the beginning?
> Have you not understood since the earth was founded?

He sits enthroned above the circle of the earth,
> and its people are like grasshoppers.

He stretches out the heavens like a canopy,
> and spreads them out like a tent to live in.

He brings princes to naught
> and reduces the rulers of this world to nothing.

No sooner are they planted,
> no sooner are they sown,
> no sooner do they take root in the ground,

than he blows on them and they wither,
> and a whirlwind sweeps them away like chaff.

'To whom will you compare me?
> Or who is my equal?' says the Holy One.

Lift up your eyes and look to the heavens:
> Who created all these?

He who brings out the starry host one by one
> and calls forth each of them by name.

Because of his great power and mighty strength,
> not one of them is missing.

(Isaiah 40:21–26)

Why is Jesus Christ the only person who is worthy to open and explain the scroll [in Revelation 5]? What is it about the Lamb of God that uniquely qualifies him to interpret it? Clearly it is because he was slain, and because of what he achieved by his death. But what is it about the cross that makes it the key to history?

First, the cross illumines history because it speaks of *victory*. The reason why the Lamb was able to open the scroll is because he has triumphed (5:5) . . . Thus the cross is represented . . . as victory not defeat, as triumph not tragedy. For, as Paul wrote, on the cross Christ dethroned and disarmed the principalities and powers of evil, triumphing over them in the cross (Col. 2:15). True, they are still alive and active, for they have not yet conceded defeat. Nevertheless, they have been conquered and are under Christ's feet (e.g. Eph. 1:22). This is the great truth of *Christus Victor*, which the church has sometimes forgotten. The first reason why the Lamb alone can interpret history with all its evil is that he triumphed over evil at the cross.

Secondly, the cross illumines history because it speaks of *redemption*. The repeated use of the title 'the Lamb' will immediately have reminded Jewish readers of the Passover. For just as the Passover lamb was sacrificed, its blood sprinkled and the people spared, so Christ our Passover has been sacrificed for us, so that we might be redeemed and might celebrate the festival of redemption. Thus, history has a twofold plot-line. There is world history (the rise and fall of empires) and there is salvation history (the story of the redeemed people of God). Moreover, we dare to say that the former is explicable only in the light of the latter; that what God is doing against the backdrop of world history is to call out from every nation a people for himself; and that only the cross makes this possible.

Thirdly, the cross illumines history because it speaks of *suffering*. For the sufferings of the Christ, although unique in their redemptive significance, were nevertheless the prototype of the sufferings of the people of God. Because he suffered, his people are called to suffer. Because he went to the cross, he calls us to take up our cross and follow him. So John moves on from the Lamb slain (in ch. 5) to the souls of the martyrs, slain because of their faithful testimony (in ch. 6). Thus those who are called to suffer for Christ, whose sufferings are so hard to understand and to bear, learn to see them in the light of the sufferings of Christ.

Fourthly, the cross illumines history because it speaks of *weakness*, and specifically of power through weakness. This paradox is seen in its most dramatic form in Christ and the cross, and in John's vision in Revelation 4 and 5. For at the centre of God's throne (symbol of power) stands a slain Lamb (symbol of weakness). In other words, power through weakness, dramatized in God on the cross and the Lamb on the throne, lies at the heart of ultimate reality, even of the mystery of almighty God himself.

John Stott, *The Incomparable Christ*, pp. 185–187

Monday
God's world-governing word

Bible reading: Psalm 33

We all know about the worldwide web. But is there such a thing as
a worldwide word? A truth for all cultures and all histories?

This psalm says that, yes there is. It is the word of God – Yahweh
God – who is Creator, Redeemer, Ruler and Judge. And for those
reasons, celebrated in verses 4–15, the psalm comes in with praise
(verses 1–3) and goes out with hope (verses 20–22). Isn't that what
all our worship should be like?

God's word will put the world to rights (verses 4–5)

'Right . . . true . . . faithful . . . righteousness . . . justice . . . unfailing
love.' Those are gospel words. Powerful words. They tell the good
news of God's character and God's Word that will ultimately
transform the world from the opposites that we find everywhere:
lies, deception, injustice, hatred . . .

Let's ask the psalmist some questions.

'How do you know that your God Yahweh is like this?'
I think he would say, come and sit down and let me tell you the story
of the exodus, when Yahweh proved his faithfulness to his promise
to Abraham, his justice against the oppressor, and his compassion
and love for us suffering slaves. We Israelites know our God from
our own history. And since Yahweh is the only God there is, then,
we conclude, this must be true for the whole earth. I know it's a
massive claim: the imagination of faith, really. But God's trans-
forming word will put all things right for all the world (verse 5).

'But how can you be sure,' we persist, *'that your God will be **able** to do all this?'*

God's word spoke the world into existence (verses 6–9)

Sit down again, our patient psalmist says. I need to take you further back. For our Scriptures do not begin with Exodus, but in Genesis. The God who delivered us from slavery is the God who created the universe – by his simple say-so. Stars, oceans, the earth – all from the command of his word. The God who had the power to make the world has the power to change the world, don't you think? But there's more. It's not just that he made the world; he rules it.

God's word governs the world according to his plans (verses 10–11)

God did not back off after creating the world. No, he is not only Lord of creation, but also Lord of history. Haven't you read the rest of our story? Empires come and go, nations rise and fall, but the plans that God spoke through his prophets stand firm. God keeps his word. God fulfils his purposes. Our God is sovereign over the stories of all nations on earth. You need to get hold of that truth in your own troublesome times, my friend.

'Really?' We want to get this clear. *'Are you saying your God knows what's going on everywhere in the world? You think he even cares about everybody in it?'*

God's word calls the world to account (verses 13–15)

Exactly and absolutely, comes the reply from our psalmist. He is the God who looks and sees and watches and considers. He does so for every person on earth – not just their actions, but their thoughts and motives too. He knows the sin of the sinner and the pain of the sinned against. Every human being is accountable to God, known by God, loved by God, matters to God. If that were not true, would there be any gospel for you to proclaim?

'But listen, one more question please. How on earth do you know this – that God sees, knows and judges every single person – even the nobodies?'

There are no nobodies to God, my friend. So many stories, so little time. Remember Hagar? A foreigner. A slave. A woman. And abominably treated and thrown out with her son to die in the desert. Who found her and saved her? Not the gods of Egypt where she came from, but the God of Abraham. And what did she say? She is the first person in our Scriptures to give God a name: 'El Roi. You are the God *who sees me.*' *Me!* A nobody? But not to God. Or there's Hannah. Or David. He knew God could see him. Reassuring in Psalm 139; not so comfortable in Psalm 51.

> *'You are a very blessed nation, to have such a God as this and to know all this about him'* (see verse 12).
>
> We are indeed. That's why we remind ourselves where our salvation comes from – and where it *doesn't* come from (verses 16–17). And that's why, if you'll excuse me, I'm going to finish my song now with words of hope and faith in the God we've been talking about. I encourage you to join in. You'll find my closing prayer in your verses 20–21. (Together then, out loud, after me...)

Tuesday
The throne of God and the Son of Man

Bible reading: Daniel 7:1–27

Empires come and empires go, but God remains sovereign, said the psalmist yesterday.

But what if you're right in the midst of one? Or in between the present one and the next? That's where Daniel was, according to the date he gives (verse 1). With Belshazzar, the Babylonian Empire's days were numbered, and Daniel probably sensed it already (see chapter 5). He had served Nebuchadnezzar's empire for a lifetime. But if it was collapsing, what would come next?

The dreams
Sequence of beasts (verses 1–8)
Fear of the future can give you bad dreams. Daniel's mind went back to Nebuchadnezzar's dream of the great statue made of four metals (Daniel 2). Only this time they have become four beasts, lumbering out of the great sea – which, for Israel, stood for the chaotic realm of evil. Three more empires will follow Babylon's, it seems, with the last the worst of all. Now, in chronological terms, the fourth may be the Greek Seleucid kingdom of the second century BC, which persecuted the Jews horrendously under Antiochus IV Epiphanes. Christian interpreters very early on identified the fourth beast, however, with the crushing teeth of the Roman Empire.

I think you'll find it more helpful, though, to see here not merely identifiable empires of the biblical era but a recurring pattern throughout history. Empires rise and fall, but sometimes especially vicious regimes arise that seem to concentrate bestial and satanic evil to a peak. This fourth beast represents such overwhelming manifestations of evil: anti-God, anti-human forces that exude arrogance, breathe out violence, devastate and destroy on an enormous scale, inflicting intense and devouring suffering on the people of God at such times. That description fits more than one regime in the past, the present and doubtless in the future too. Jews and Christians can fill in the blanks only too tragically.

Split-screen vision (verses 9–12)

Suddenly Daniel's dream changes, as dreams do. He sees a blazingly bright heavenly throne room, and he sees One on the throne who is obviously the Lord God – with the ageless authority of eternity itself. God is still on the throne! But here's the thing. This picture does not *replace* the earlier one. For Daniel is still watching what is happening in the realm of the fourth beast and its boastful horn (verses 11–12). This is like split-screen technology. Daniel can see an upper portion (the government of God) and a lower portion (the rampaging beasts). *And they are both going on at the same time.* Daniel is seeing two realities, heavenly and earthly, but both are dimensions of the same picture. God reigns in and over the world of 'the beasts'.

And here's another thing – most reassuring. This is not just a *throne*, the seat of government. It is a *court*, the seat of judgment (last lines of verse 10). So the beasts are not in control – or out of control, for that matter. No, they are subject to the permission and authority of the Judge of all the earth. The books are being written; nothing will escape the record or be swept under the carpet. All wrongdoing will face God's justice, and all bestial power will ultim-ately be stripped and destroyed (verses 11–12). Good news or what?

Son of Man and saints (verses 13–14, 18, 26–27)

But who is this? Daniel's dream morphs once more and he sees, in the midst of all that blazing divine glory and the clouds of heaven . . . a human! He'd seen beasts 'like a lion, like a bear, like a leopard', but now, after all those images of distorted and destructive creatures, 'one like a man'. God's victory, God's authority, God's indestructible kingdom, will be in the hands of this one, a son of man (verses 13–14). The promise of Genesis 3:15 will be fulfilled. God will destroy the serpent's power through the seed of Eve. Humanity will be restored to its rightful rule within creation (Hebrews 1:5–9). Radical reconciliation indeed!

Of course, we know who this Son of Man is, for he claimed the title for himself (a claim which clinched his crucifixion: Matthew 26:63–66). And his destiny is ours, for the explanation given to Daniel identifies the Son of Man with the saints – the holy people of God. Like him, we suffer. And with him, we shall reign. Revelation completes the picture.

Verse 28 is hardly surprising! But 8:27 is my favourite verse in Daniel. After such visions, 'I got up and went about the king's business.' He went back to work! Back to the office, back to his day job.

Will you go to work today with the spiritual perception, like Daniel's, to recognize the evil and satanic power that lurks behind human structures, and, at the same time, having the faith in God's sovereign governance and ultimate justice that enables you to go on living and serving in his world? Pray for such discernment, wisdom and faith.

Wednesday
'To fulfil what the Lord said through the prophets'

Bible reading: Matthew 1:18 – 2:18

What's this? Christmas in the middle of Lent? Haven't we landed at the wrong end of the Gospels here?

Bear with me, please! What we're thinking about this week is God the Sovereign Governor of history, and we're coming to the part where we see how he exercises that supremely through the Lord Jesus Christ and his death, resurrection and ascension. But Matthew wants us to see that even in Jesus' birth and infancy, God was showing his control of events. God is doing what Psalm 33:11 told us, fulfilling the plans he had declared through the word of the prophets. Or, as Paul puts it, 'When the set time had fully come, God sent his Son, born of a woman . . .' (Galatians 4:4).

Jesus completes the story

Actually, Matthew makes this point in the way he begins his Gospel, with those first seventeen verses that you're probably glad I didn't ask you to read (and have never heard read at any Christmas carol service I've been to). What Matthew is doing in his long genealogy of Jesus is saying to his readers, 'You won't understand this Jesus unless you see him as the destination of *this* story – the story of our people, of our God, in our Scriptures.' And that story, we know, was the story of God's sovereign perseverance through all the generations of Israel since his promise to Abraham – three times double seven generations (1:17), a scheme intended to express God's perfect control. God governs the very moment of Jesus' arrival.

Jesus fulfils the promise

If you think of the story underlying Matthew's genealogy as a *journey*, then Jesus is not only the *destination* but also *the whole point* of that journey. He fulfils its purpose. He gives it meaning. He is why it all happened. The whole journey/story is there in our Bibles because God, in his sovereign governance of history, was planning for this moment – the arrival of his Son, the Messiah, Jesus of Nazareth.

That is what Matthew is getting at, with his four quotations from the Old Testament that he says were 'fulfilled' in his early narrative (well, actually there's a fifth, in 2:23, but nobody is completely sure which text Matthew has in mind there).

- *Immanuel* (1:22): the virgin conception and birth of Jesus reminds Matthew of the sign that Isaiah gave to Ahaz (Isaiah 7:14), promising God's deliverance because 'God is with us'.
- *Bethlehem* (2:5–6): the scripture scholars gave the Magi the right answer as to where the king of the Jews would come from (to Herod's great alarm), quoting Micah 5:2.
- *Egypt* (2:14–15): 'Israel is my firstborn son,' God had said while they were in Egypt (Exodus 4:22). Then God called his son out of Egypt. And Matthew sees even the temporary refugee status of God's Son, Jesus, in Egypt as a re-enactment of that exodus moment, as recalled by Hosea (Hosea 11:1).
- *Exile* (2:17–18): the grief of the mothers in Bethlehem reminds Matthew of Jeremiah imagining Rachel weeping (in her grave, of course) as the exiles trudged past from shattered Jerusalem (Jeremiah 31:15). He may have meant us to remember, though, that the very next verse promises they will return.

What is Matthew doing here? This is not just a tick-box list of *predictions* that Jesus has managed to make come true. Indeed, only one (Micah's about Bethlehem) is really a long-term prediction at all. Immanuel was a meaningful sign to Ahaz (and Joseph and Mary called their son Jesus, not Immanuel). Hosea was talking about the past. Jeremiah is lamenting something he himself lived through. So what's it all about?

Matthew sees the whole Old Testament as declaring God's covenant commitment to his people Israel, and through Israel to all the nations of the world. He sees God governing history in order to keep that commitment. And Jesus, as Messiah, embodied and represented Israel. So everything about Jesus simply 'fits' that great promise, completes that great journey, proves God's sovereignty. That's why Matthew piles up these quotations from the prophets around his arrival.

The Radical Reconciler arrives according to plan.

Of course, it's far too soon to get ready for Christmas, but it's never too soon to give thanks to God that every part of Jesus' life, from conception to ascension, declares the sovereignty of God in history.

The plans of the LORD stand firm for ever,
    the purposes of his heart through all generations.
(Psalm 33:11)

It's not so much a question of 'How can I apply this story to my own life?' as 'How can I place my life today within this great story of God and play my part in his purposes for the world in my generation?'

Thursday
'By God's deliberate plan'

Bible reading: Acts 2:14–41

Imagine yourself as one of the crowd in Jerusalem on the day of Pentecost. You've stayed on after the Passover, just seven weeks ago. And you vividly remember that torrid week.

You were among the crowds cheering that prophet from Nazareth, Jesus they called him, as he rode into Jerusalem. You were fooled by the crowd's hysteria into thinking he was the Messiah who would rid the country of the Romans, with everybody waving palm branches, the symbol of Jewish independence, to support him. But he completely let the side down, didn't he? Total failure. The authorities were right; he *was* a real threat, but not to the Romans, to us Jews, as if we hadn't got enough troubles. So you joined the mob yelling for him to be crucified. Quite right. Blaspheming impostor! He had to go.

But what's all this commotion this morning? There's a small bunch of men talking loudly outside a building, and, hey! You suddenly realize one of them is speaking your own native language from Cyprus. Some friends you've made from Rome call out to you, 'They're speaking Latin over here!' You catch bits from the praise psalms. All about the wonders God has done. What wonders? It's wild and noisy. Have they been drinking!?

Then one of them – Peter, you later discover – raises his voice with a Big Speech. 'What you're seeing and hearing is what the prophet Joel said would happen,' he starts, and goes on to reel off a long quote about God pouring out his Spirit in the last days. What, really? Now? What's happened to bring this about? Then he's off again: 'Listen up!'

'You'll remember Jesus of Nazareth . . .' (Not him again! Could you ever forget?) Peter goes on, 'You put him to death, didn't you? You had him spiked on a cross. Yes, it was by the wicked hands of unclean Gentiles, but you're as guilty as they are.' That's uncomfortable. Peter's making it sound like unjustified murder.

'But God has raised him from the dead!'

Horrors! Now you're really scared. There's only one reason a murdered man would come back to life – for vengeance on his killers. This doesn't sound like the good news and wonders of God they were hollering about a moment ago.

But Peter is saying something astonishing, something that turns the whole thing upside down. *'This all happened by God's deliberate plan and foreknowledge.* Yes, you did it and you meant it. You crucified him, and it was unspeakably evil. But God planned it from the beginning.' And then Peter is off quoting more scriptures from David, about how God would never abandon his Messiah in the grave, and how all these guys had actually *seen* Jesus alive again – in person. Incredible! They've seen him. They've touched him. They've had meals with him – the one you saw mangled and dead on that cross . . .

Your head is spinning with this. That terrible Friday, that awful crucifixion, was all part of God's plan? Not to get rid of a *false* messiah (as you all thought), but to have the *true* Messiah put to death? God was in charge all along? And God had reversed the injustice of it by raising Jesus from the dead, demonstrating to you and all the world that this Jesus, whom you helped to crucify, truly is Messiah and Lord? Peter spells it out, loud and emphatic (verse 36). God has done this! Cross *and* resurrection. This is all God's work. This was always God's plan.

But what could you do? You were part of the crowd that wanted him crucified. Could God ever forgive you? Everybody's asking the same question. And Peter isn't finished.

'Yes of course! Don't you see? That's the whole point. Turn back to God. Be baptized [like John did, only in the name of Jesus the Messiah], and, sure, your sins will be forgiven – even the greatest sin you or anybody could have committed – and you too will receive the gift of the Holy Spirit. This is his day. Come and join the party!'

So you do. You and a few thousand others in Jerusalem that amazing day. But you can't wait to get back to Cyprus to tell your family what you've seen and heard in Jerusalem, and to share the good news of Jesus, crucified and risen, Messiah and Lord, with your fellow Jews there, and anybody else for that matter.

Ponder the mystery of the cross today in the light of Acts 2:23. This was the greatest act of human and satanic evil in the history of the cosmos. Yet simultaneously, within the sovereign plan of God from eternity, it was the greatest act of divine goodness and grace. Here is the moment that echoes, but infinitely surpasses, Joseph's word to his brothers (Genesis 50:20).

When we struggle to cope with the evil and suffering in our world, we must eventually come to the foot of the cross and strive to hold these three vast biblical truths together: the utter wickedness of evil; the utter sovereignty of God; and the utter redeeming power of the cross.

Friday
'All authority in heaven and on earth'

Bible reading: Luke 24:44–53; Matthew 28:16–20

Let's recap. On Wednesday we saw how the account of the *birth and infancy* of Christ declared the sovereign control of God over the whole story of the Bible so far. Even the timing was just right, for it was set by God himself, as Paul said (Galatians 4:4). And yesterday we listened to Peter affirming the same truth about the *death* of Christ. The cross itself was entirely within the plan of God, the supreme act of his governance of history (Acts 2:23).

Today, however, we are in the presence of the *risen* Christ, first on the evening of the day of resurrection (in Luke 24), and then on the Mount of Ascension (in Matthew 28). And we find the same truth affirmed. But it is not only that the resurrection of Christ is an act of God's sovereign power in itself. For Christ not only is risen, but also is ascended to the right hand of God. Which means that God continues to exercise his sovereign rule over human history *through* the Lord Jesus Christ – crucified, risen and ascended. (And tomorrow we shall rejoice that it is the Lamb who was slain who is the Lamb on the throne.)

Messiah and mission (Luke 24:44–49)

Wouldn't you love to have been able to listen in on the two Resurrection Lectures that Jesus gave on his first day out of the tomb? (As an Old Testament teacher, I've always found it encouraging that Jesus spent most of the first day of his risen life teaching

121

the Scriptures!) First, in the afternoon on the road to Emmaus (24:25–27), and then in the evening in the upper room.

'This is what is written,' he said (verse 46). If you had been there, pencil and paper at the ready, you might have asked, 'Excuse me, Lord, but where exactly is this written? Could we have chapter and verse, please?' But Jesus isn't quoting particular verses. He is summarizing the message of the whole Old Testament. This is what it's all about, what it's all pointing towards, or 'This is what God always planned, as he revealed in his Word'.

But Jesus doesn't just point to the immediate events as the fulfilment of Scripture – that is, what has just happened to him as Messiah, in his death and resurrection (verse 46). God's scripture plan, he continues, points beyond Easter and Pentecost to the ongoing mission of the church (verse 47). And that includes you and me. Of course, Jesus meant that his first disciples would be his primary witnesses (verse 48). But the task of bringing the gospel to all nations (God keeping his promise to Abraham) involves God's people in every generation.

Are you in the team? Is your church?

'The Great Commission' (Matthew 28:18–20)

Jesus's words at the end of Matthew's Gospel are often quoted as the mandate for the church's mission. Jesus starts not with a command, however, but with an affirmation: *'All authority in heaven and on earth has been given to me.'* Knowing their Scriptures, the disciples would have heard a clear echo of Moses: 'Acknowledge and take to heart this day that the LORD is God in heaven above and on the earth below. There is no other' (Deuteronomy 4:39). 'Heaven and earth' was the typical Jewish way of speaking of all creation. It's where the Bible begins (Genesis 1:1) and where it ends (Revelation 21:1). And here, in the middle of the story, the crucified and risen Christ claims the authority of the Creator himself over the whole cosmos. No wonder both Matthew and Luke tell us 'they worshipped him' (though Matthew is honest enough to say that some doubted). Jews though they were, they knew they were in the presence of the Lord God of Israel.

What does all this mean for you and me? It means that, as we go out into the world every day, we are walking on Christ's property. For 'the earth is the Lord's', as both the psalmist and Paul say (Psalm 24:1; 1 Corinthians 10:26). And if you claim to love someone, you take care of their property.

It also means that, wherever we go in the world for the sake of the gospel, we go with Christ's authority. There is not an inch of the planet that belongs to any other power or god. Our mandate to make disciples of all nations comes from the Lord of all creation.

> 'Mission is an inescapable deduction from the cosmic Lordship of Christ,' John Stott used to say.
>
> Do we get so familiar with thinking of Jesus as 'my Lord' in personal terms that we don't think through the wider missional implications of that opening announcement of the Great Commission? How do you respond to the Lausanne Movement's statement?
>
> > 'If Jesus is Lord of all the earth, we cannot separate our relationship to Christ from how we act in relation to the earth. For to proclaim the gospel that says "Jesus is Lord" is to proclaim the gospel that includes the earth, since Christ's Lordship is over all creation. Creation care is a thus a gospel issue within the Lordship of Christ.'
> > (*The Cape Town Commitment* I.7.a)

Saturday
The slain Lamb
is on the throne[1]

Bible reading: Revelation 5:1 – 6:8

The four horsemen of the apocalypse! What sort of way is that to end the week? But please bear with me. There is good news ahead. It's a very long reading today, but really, we have to see Revelation 4 – 7 as one whole connected vision, so I've actually cut it short for you!

The Lamb with the plan

Remember Daniel's split-screen vision in Daniel 7? Something similar happens in Revelation 4. John sees the throne room of heaven, the seat of government of the whole universe, including the world John himself lives in, and our world. Then, in chapter 5, John sees that the living God on the throne holds a sealed scroll, which seems to stand for the meaning and purpose of history, the great plan of God for all time. But it is sealed with seven seals. Who is worthy to govern history, to interpret and carry out the plan of God? The answer comes, 'The Lamb who was slain!', which means, of course, the crucified Jesus. So John now sees the crucified and risen Jesus sharing the very throne of God and taking the scroll and opening it, seal by seal (5:5–7). Jesus, the Lamb of God, holds the scroll of God's purpose, the key to the meaning and goal of all history.

---

1 Some of today's reflection is adapted from a chapter in my book *The God I Don't Understand: Reflections on Tough Questions of Faith* (Grand Rapids, Mich.: Zondervan, 2008), chapter 3, 'The Defeat of Evil'.

The Lamb who was slain

Why is Jesus worthy to open the scroll? The song of Revelation 5:9–10 gives three crucially important reasons, all focused on the cross.

- Because he was slain, and through his death 'purchased' people for God. The cross is *redemptive.*
- Because through his death Jesus fulfilled God's purpose, ever since Abraham, to bless people from *every* nation. The cross is *universal.*
- Because through his death Jesus has achieved victory for his people, who will reign with him on the earth. The cross is *victory.* The Lamb wins!

So the unfolding and meaning of history flow from the cross, just as the scroll unrolls in the hands of the Lamb who was slain. We have to look at the world from the perspective of the cross of Christ and all that it accomplished.

The horsemen of history

So the scroll starts to unroll, seal by seal, and the opening of the first four seals shocks us even further. What on earth is going on here? These horses and their riders are probably symbolic of realities in John's own day (and ours). They portray disasters that we see in repeated cycles all through human history.

- The white horse speaks of invasion and conquest, through bow and crown.[2]
- The red horse speaks of war, probably civil war and rebellion especially, in which people slaughter one another.
- The black horse speaks of famine, or rather famine for some but continuing luxuries for others.
- The pale horse speaks of disease, plague, epidemic and death of all kinds.

2 Some interpreters take the white horse as meaning Christ himself, by comparison with Revelation 19:11–15. Christ leads the parade, as it were, demonstrating his sovereignty over all that follows. I prefer my own interpretation!

Now these are constant realities of life on earth. These four horse-men are not apocalyptic nightmares of the distant future. These four riders thunder through the pages of every history book of every era. We can see the horsemen of conquest, war, famine and disease in multiple forms all over the world today.

And what about John's own day? Here are just some of the terrible events that had convulsed the Roman Empire during the last thirty-five or so years of John's life:

- earthquakes in AD 60;
- the fire of Rome in AD 64 and the persecution of Christians that followed;
- the four-year horror of the Jewish war, which ended in the destruction of Jerusalem and the temple in AD 70;
- the suicide of Nero in AD 68, followed by chaos, civil war and four rival claimants to the throne;
- the obliterating eruption of the volcano Vesuvius in AD 79;
- a serious grain famine in AD 92.

Who is in control?

But here's the thing. John sees the horsemen ride out from the scroll *in the hand of the Lamb*. That is to say, 'John's vision of the four horsemen is intended to assert Christ's sovereignty over such a world as that.' Indeed, 'unless Christ can be said to reign over the world of hard facts in which Christians must live their lives, he can hardly be said to reign at all' (George B. Caird, *Revelation*, p. 79).

But wait! Is this all there is to the reign of Christ? Nothing more than a kind of cosmic supervision of devouring evils rampaging out of control?

Ah, but that is precisely the point. They are *not* out of control.

Who summons them? Notice the word 'Come'. Each one is summoned under the sovereign authority of the throne. God rules the world, not the horsemen.

Who gives them power? Notice that to each of them something 'was given' (e.g. a bow, a sword). This is a way of saying that they do have power, but it is temporary, provisional, subject to God's right to give and take away.

And above all, who is opening the seals? The Lamb who was slain! The crucified Christ is in charge of the unfolding of history within which these horrors take place.
Caird, *Revelation*, pp. 82–83; my italics)

The Lamb who was slain is the one who holds and opens the scroll. It was by his death on the cross that Jesus became worthy, that is, gained the right, to open the scroll. This means (and this is the absolutely vital point to grasp) that *Christ's power to control these evil forces is the same power as the power he exercised on the cross.*

And what was that power? Remember our reflection on 'the paradox of power' at the cross, on the Friday after Ash Wednesday? We are seeing it here again.

The cross was the worst that human evil and rebellion against God could do. There was a cocktail of inflamed fanatics, corrupt religious leaders, lying witnesses, political conspiracy, vested interests, nationalist rage, morally bankrupt judicial process, excruciating torture, public shame and taunting mockery. And even among the friends of Jesus there were treachery, betrayal, denial and cowardice. And, at a more profound level, we know that all the powers of satanic evil were ranged against Christ and hurled their worst at him.

Divine judo

But Jesus, the Lamb of God, turned all this around into the triumph of divine love, absorbing and defeating it simultaneously. But here's another crucial thing: not only did Jesus defeat all the powers of evil, he made them into the agents of their own defeat. *He turned evil against itself, to its own ultimate destruction.*

In the sport of judo, so I'm told, the essential idea is to take all the energy and force of your opponent's attack and turn it back on them in such a way that they are flattened by their own assault. If it is not too irreverent to put it like this, the cross was God's supreme judo throw. In the person of his Son, he took all that sin and evil, human and satanic, could hurl at him – and turned it back to its own ultimate destruction.

The Lamb who was slain is the Lamb on the throne

That, then, was the reality of the cross – the central moment in human history when God dealt with evil. (Remember Week 1?) *But now*, says John, *that same Jesus, the Lamb who was slain, reigns over the forces of evil that are loose in our world, in the same way as he reigned from the cross*. Ultimately, all that is evil and destructive will be brought under the sovereign power of the cross, to its own final destruction.

I quoted from George Caird's commentary earlier. Here is the climax of what he has to say about Revelation 5:

> The point is that, just where sin and its effects are most in evidence, the kingship of the Crucified is to be seen, turning human wickedness to the service of God's purpose. The heavenly voice which says **'Come!'** is not calling disasters into existence. They are to be found in any case, wherever there are cruelty, selfishness, ambition, lust, greed, fear and pride. Rather the voice is declaring that *nothing can now happen, not even the most fearsome evidence of man's disobedience and its nemesis, which cannot be woven into the pattern of God's gracious purpose* ... The content of the scroll is God's redemptive plan, by which he brings good out of evil and makes everything on earth subservient to his sovereignty.[3]

Revelation 5 – 7, then, affirms this awesome paradox, which is crucial to the way we should think about the evils of history. All

---

3   Caird, *Revelation*, pp. 82–83 (my italics).

evil, disaster and suffering stand under the sovereign control of God in Christ – and specifically under the authority of the crucified Christ (the Lamb who was slain, who is in the centre of the throne, sharing in the government of God over all creation). The first four seals (the horsemen) are as much under God's sovereignty as the destiny of the martyrs (fifth seal, 6:9–11), the judgment of the wicked (sixth seal, 6:12–17) and the salvation of God's people from all nations (7:1–17, especially 9–10).

Now I'm sure you believe that God is in sovereign charge of the protection of his people, the judgment of the wicked and the salvation of people from all nations. Well then, Jesus summons us, through this vision given to John, to believe that he is just as surely Sovereign over the very things that most seem to threaten those plans. The Lamb who was slain *is* on the throne!

We finish our week with awestruck humility, reflecting on this vision: that God's sovereignty is exercised by the same one (the crucified Christ), and in the same way (through the paradoxical power of the cross), to the very end of history.

The cross showed us that God could take the worst possible evil and through it accomplish the greatest possible good – the destruction of evil itself. In the light of that, under the governance of the Crucified, nothing can happen in human history over which God is not ultimately Sovereign, and which he cannot, though his infinite power and wisdom, weave into the outworking of his universal purpose of redeeming love for the whole creation.

Holy Week

CREATION RESTORED

Palm Sunday
Rejoicing and weeping over Jerusalem

Rejoice greatly, Daughter Zion!
 Shout, Daughter Jerusalem!
See, your king comes to you,
 righteous and victorious,
lowly and riding on a donkey,
 on a colt, the foal of a donkey.
I will take away the chariots from Ephraim
 and the war-horses from Jerusalem,
 and the battle-bow will be broken.
He will proclaim peace to the nations.
 His rule will extend from sea to sea
 and from the River to the ends of the earth.
(Zechariah 9:9–10)

After Jesus had said this, he went on ahead, going up to Jerusalem. As he approached Bethphage and Bethany at the hill called the Mount of Olives, he sent two of his disciples, saying to them, 'Go to the village ahead of you, and as you enter it, you will find a colt tied there, which no one has ever ridden. Untie it and bring it here. If anyone asks you, "Why are you untying it?" say, "The Lord needs it."'

Those who were sent ahead went and found it just as he had told them. As they were untying the colt, its owners asked them, 'Why are you untying the colt?'

They replied, 'The Lord needs it.'

They brought it to Jesus, threw their cloaks on the colt and put Jesus on it. As he went along, people spread their cloaks on the road.

When he came near the place where the road goes down the Mount of Olives, the whole crowd of disciples began joyfully to praise God in loud voices for all the miracles they had seen:

'Blessed is the king who comes in the name of the Lord!'

'Peace in heaven and glory in the highest!'

Some of the Pharisees in the crowd said to Jesus, 'Teacher, rebuke your disciples!'

'I tell you,' he replied, 'if they keep quiet, the stones will cry out.'

As he approached Jerusalem and saw the city, he wept over it and said, 'If you, even you, had only known on this day what would bring you peace – but now it is hidden from your eyes. The days will come upon you when your enemies will build an embankment against you and encircle you and hem you in on every side. They will dash you to the ground, you and the children within your walls. They will not leave one stone on another, because you did not recognize the time of God's coming to you.'
(Luke 19:28–44)

As Jesus approached Jerusalem and saw the city, he wept over it.
(Luke 19:41)

Jesus's entry into Jerusalem is recorded by all four evangelists, although each adds details that the others omit. Jesus had evidently made up his mind to fulfil what stood written of him in Zechariah 9, namely that a future king of Judah would ride into Jerusalem bringing salvation, yet not with swashbuckling bravado nor on a prancing warhorse, but humbly and meekly on the back (of all creatures!) of a donkey. Thus he would 'proclaim peace to the nations' (Zech. 9:10).

This incident bears all the signs of having been prearranged and even stage managed. Probably on a previous visit Jesus had arranged with friends in Bethany to lend him their donkey, releasing on the agreed password, 'The Master needs it.' Then the crowds entered into the drama, spreading their clothes on the donkey's back and on the road and breaking into spontaneous cheering.

Having passed through the villages of Bethany and Bethphage, the cavalcade rounded the brow of the Mount of Olives, and suddenly Jerusalem came into view, with its glittering pinnacles and the spacious courts of the temple. Here, it seems, as the shouts of the crowd died down, to everybody's astonishment and embarrassment Jesus burst into tears. Through his sobs he uttered a prophetic lament over the city, predicting its destruction because it did not recognize the time of God's visitation.

It is surely remarkable that, at the very moment when Jesus warned the city of judgment, he was weeping over it in love. Divine judgment (which is the main theme throughout Holy Week) is a solemn, awesome reality. But the God who judges is the God who weeps. He is not willing that any should perish. And when in the end his judgment falls on anybody (as Jesus said it will), God's eyes will be full of tears.

John Stott, *Through the Bible through the Year*, p. 224

Monday
Curse and covenant

Bible reading: Genesis 5:28–29; 9:7–17

Our problem

What's the big problem, the one afflicting the human race, to which we need a big solution? Well, it's sin, you answer, and I agree. But the question I'm asking here is this: 'Isn't there an even bigger problem?'

One very common description of the problem goes like this: how can we humans who have been sinful and rebellious ever since the fall come into the presence of the holy God? And, especially, how can God let us into his sinless heaven when we are so full of sin? How can we get to go and be with God? 'Your iniquities have separated you from your God,' we quote (Isaiah 59:2), assuming that they stop *us* getting to *him*.

God coming here

Of course, sometimes the Bible does talk in this way. Peter says that Jesus died on the cross 'to bring us to God' (1 Peter 3:18). And through the blood of Jesus, we are brought near to God and have access to his presence (Ephesians 2:13, 18). These are precious and wonderful truths. But in the early chapters of Genesis, that is not how the problem is presented. There, it is not so much a question of how we can get to go and live with God some time in the future – after death is not even contemplated – but how we can get God to come back and live with us here on the earth he created and where he placed us.

'Oh, that you would rend the heavens and come down' (Isaiah 64:1) would perhaps fit better in terms of who needs to go where.

And it is how the Bible will end, with the ultimate cry of 'Immanuel': God dwelling with us – at last (Revelation 21:3).

Give us a break!

So when Lamech (the descendant of Seth, not the one descended from Cain, 4:19–24) fathers a son, he gives him a name that means 'Comfort' or 'Rest' – Noah. And the longing of his heart probably expresses the longing that the whole chapter of passing generations has produced: 'He will comfort us in the labour and painful toil of our hands caused by the ground the LORD has cursed' (Genesis 5:29). He is clearly echoing Genesis 3:17–19.

God's curse in response to Adam's disobedience explicitly includes both a negative impact on the ground itself (only by toil and sweat will humans survive on it) and the verdict that our lives will end in the dust of death. Genesis 5 has tolled the bell of death every few verses. No matter how long anybody lives, it all ends up with 'and then he died'. The repetition triggers Lamech's longing. If only God would do something about the curse. If only God would reverse for us the effects of the fall. If only . . . And God did indeed plan to do just that, but not in Lamech's son's time.

The covenant with Noah

Noah did, however, see a kind of relaunch of God's creation project. After the flood, God renews to Noah the words of blessing first spoken to the human race (9:1, 7). And then God makes his emphatic, rainbow-wrapped, covenant promise. On the one hand, God says he will never again curse the earth in the form of a destructive flood (8:21; 9:11).[1] Rather, on the other hand, God makes a solemn covenant with the earth itself and every living creature on it (8:22; 9:8–17). Notice how often God insists that this is a covenant not just with the human race but with 'all life on earth'. God loves his creation!

---

1 That does not preclude that God will finally bring judgment on the whole earth. 2 Peter 3 sees the 'destroying' waters of the flood as a prototype of the 'fire' of God's final judgment, which, like the flood, should be seen as God purging and cleansing the whole earth, not obliterating it altogether. What will be destroyed is not the creation itself, but the sinful human and satanic world order that has polluted it.

Suffering creation

But still creation remains subject to the frustration and futility of the curse, groaning and longing for liberation from its bondage to decay, as Paul points out (Romans 8:19–21). Creation is further marred by our sin, and all the destructive effects of human violence and greed, ignorance and folly. The Bible is not unaware of the damage that humans do to the earth – far from it. Our social wickedness causes creational grief (Hosea 4:1–3). War especially is so destructive of nature that God pronounces a severe 'Woe' on those who perpetrate the damage, such as the Babylonians (Habakkuk 2:17; 'Lebanon' means the trees – the famous cedars of Lebanon, in parallel with the animals).

Since the scale of the problem is huge, God's answer will need to be correspondingly comprehensive. The rest of the Bible story, centred on the cross and climaxing in new creation, assures us that indeed it is.

How big is your gospel? How big is the problem it addresses?

Let Genesis expand your answer. This week we celebrate how God addressed the brokenness of Genesis 3, 4 – 5 and 11.

'The gospel is God's good news, through the cross and resurrection of Jesus Christ, for individual persons, *and* for society, *and* for creation. All three are broken and suffering because of sin; all three are included in the redeeming love and mission of God; all three must be part of the comprehensive mission of God's people.'
(*The Cape Town Commitment* 1.7.a)

Tuesday
Let the earth be glad

Bible reading: Psalm 96:10–13; Isaiah 65:17–25

Yesterday, Paul heard the whole creation *groaning*. Today, the psalmist hears the whole creation *rejoicing*. What has made the difference?

The answer is the arrival of the kingdom of God (Psalm 96:10). Jesus announced that he had inaugurated God's reign through his own life and work. Paul taught us (in Romans 5, as we saw on Week 2 Saturday) that we live in the era of conflict between the reign of grace and life and the continuing reign of sin and death. But when God fully establishes his kingdom, then our psalmist's song will fill the universe.

So what will it be like when God reigns over all the earth? The song calls on our imagination to envisage the world as a very different place from what we know now.

How is your imagination today? Or better, how is your faith?

A world of reliability (verse 10)

The world will be stable and *firmly established*, as it was at creation. But the world we know (in the psalmist's day as much as our own) is a world of chaotic instability, among the nations and in the physical world of nature and climate.

But not for ever. God's reign will restore the world order that he decrees, and we shall be safe.

A world of righteousness (verses 10b and 13b; 'equity' means fairness)

Yet the world is bulging and collapsing under the weight of injustice, oppression and cruelty.

But not for ever. When God comes to reign, he will *put all things right*, which is what verse 13 means: *he will judge the world in righteousness and the peoples in his faithfulness.* That's good news indeed!

A world of rejoicing (verse 11)

Yet the world is filled with incalculable grief, mourning and tears, both from the mountain of human suffering and also (as we saw yesterday) from the groaning of creation itself under the devastation of human wickedness and wastefulness. Is your heart not broken at the sight of yet more starving, homeless and brutalized children? How can God bear it? God, who sees the pain of every child on earth, and every grieving parent, and every life shattered by weapons and maiming, not to mention every dying animal species, every poisoned, hunted and tangled creature, and every piece of polluted land and sea and air?

But not for ever! When God comes to reign, all creation will rejoice. The poetry soars, as we imagine the sea resounding, the fields rejoicing, the trees singing, the rivers clapping their hands and the mountains singing together (Psalm 98:8). These are poetic metaphors, but profound truth.

A world of fulfilment and safety
(Isaiah 65:17–25)

Isaiah shifts our focus from the natural order to the world of human life (though he returns to nature in verse 25). Can you see how, as we observed yesterday, Isaiah is not thinking of us going off to heaven, but of God renewing and restoring his creation, and our life within it? 'Look,' says God; 'I am creating [the form of the verb means God is in the process of doing this already] new heavens and a new earth.' Imagine, says Isaiah (far surpassing John Lennon), a world without tears (verse 19). Imagine a world without premature death (verse 20). Imagine a world without all the fruit of our labours being stolen by others (verses 21–22). Imagine a world without the suffering of children and grandchildren (verse 23). Imagine a world where God is so close that his blessing doesn't even need to be asked for (verse 24). Imagine a world where nature itself is freed from predation and harm, and where all the devil's works are as crushed as he will be (verse 25).

Rejoice today that this is not just a dream of what *might* be, but a vision and promise of what *will* be. Revelation 21 – 22 draws deeply on Isaiah's prophecy. Here is how William Cowper envisaged it:

Rivers of gladness water all the earth,
And clothe all climes with beauty. The reproach
Of barrenness is past. The fruitful field
Laughs with abundance; and the land, once lean
Or fertile only in its own disgrace,
Exults to see its thistly curse repeal'd.

One song employs all nations; and all cry,
'Worthy the Lamb, for He was slain for us!'
The dwellers in the vales and on the rocks
Shout to each other, and the mountain tops
From distant mountains catch the flying joy;
Till, nation after nation taught the strain,
Earth rolls the rapturous Hosanna round.
(From William Cowper, 'The Task', 1785)

Wednesday
Creation reconciled

Bible reading: Colossians 1:15–20

Who is this Jesus we are walking with this Holy Week? Who rode the donkey into Jerusalem on Sunday? Who will give astonishing meaning to bread and wine during the Passover meal on Thursday? Who will be tried, mocked, flogged, stripped and tortured to death on Friday?

Our hearts will go out, with hymns of love and gratitude, to this man Jesus who gave his very life for us, for us whose sin made his suffering and death the only God-ordained means of our salvation. Paul reminds us in today's reading that Jesus Christ doesn't need our sympathy, but he calls for our worship.

Jesus and the Lord God of Israel

For *this* is who he is! This is probably the most exalted piece of writing in all Paul's letters, and it may well be that Paul is quoting an early Christian hymn or creed. And at both ends Jesus is identified with the Lord God of Israel's faith: as the image of the invisible God (verse 15) and the one in whom all God's fullness dwells (verse 19). But what does it mean to identify Jesus with the God of the Old Testament in this way?

Creator and Redeemer

The Old Testament affirms that Yahweh God, the Holy One of Israel, is the Creator of the heavens and earth, and the Redeemer of both. Our readings in Genesis and Isaiah have shown us this. And Paul now boldly affirms that Jesus Christ, the Son, shares that double identity. In fact, it is Christ, as Creator and as Reconciler,

141

who holds this creation and the new creation together! Look how Paul does this.

Beginning of this creation

Our poem has two balancing halves, and the link word between them is 'firstborn' (verses 15 and 18b). Christ is the firstborn – that is, the heir – over all creation (verse 15). It was all created 'in him . . . through him . . . and for him'. Now Paul could not make it any clearer that he means the whole of the present universe. He uses the standard Jewish pairing 'heaven and earth' twice, and the equivalent term 'all things' five times in these verses. Paul is not just talking about the world of nature. He includes things 'visible and invisible, whether thrones or powers or rulers or authorities' (verse 16). That means both the invisible spiritual and demonic forces that oppose God, and the all-too-visible human powers and authorities (such as the Roman Empire in Paul's day) that easily come to embody such spiritual forces with their ideologies and idolatry. They too are part of the whole created order – and Christ is Lord over all, holding it all together, even in its fallen state.

Beginning of the new creation

Then, in the second half, Paul states that Christ is 'the firstborn from among the dead' (verse 18b). Here, Paul sees the death and resurrection of Christ as the beginning of the whole new order of things – the new creation, of which the risen Christ is the prototype and pioneer. And we, the church, stand in the middle of these two halves (verse 18a). For we still live within the old and broken creation, and share in its sin and brokenness. And yet, at the same time, we are the body of Christ and the emerging population of the new creation.

That leads Paul to his mind-stretching climax. For how did Christ achieve this amazing feat of cosmic redemption? No prizes for guessing: by his death on the cross (verse 20).

Making peace through the blood of the cross

Paul's language is rich – and subversive. God, he claims, has reconciled to himself 'all things' (and again, it is clear he means the whole creation) 'by making peace through his blood, shed on the cross'. How much the whole creation and all nations within it long for peace – in the natural and the human and the spiritual worlds! And God has done it . . . through the blood of the cross! The reconciliation that Christ accomplished on the cross is not only *radical*, reaching to the deepest roots of our need. It is *cosmic*, reaching to the farthest corners of creation in its scope and power.

Subversive? Yes, because the Roman Empire also 'made peace' by the blood of the cross. That's to say, they pacified whole regions by crucifying those who opposed them. But, as we saw in our study of Ephesians 2, God's way of making peace was by bearing in himself, in the person of his Son, all the sin, evil, enmity and rebellion – and their cost and consequences – at the cross. And in that divine act of self-giving and atoning love, God-in-Christ reconciled his whole creation.

Of all our meditations on what Jesus meant by 'It is finished', this is surely the climax. Evil and death defeated. Sinners forgiven. Enemies reconciled. History governed. *And all creation reconciled to God.* Radical Reconciler indeed! Marvel in your heart and mind at these great dimensions of God's salvation as we approach Calvary and Easter.

Maundy Thursday
The new wine of the kingdom

Bible reading: Luke 22:7–20

Lest we forget

'Do this in remembrance of me.' How often we have heard those words as we participate in the Lord's Supper, or Holy Communion, or Eucharist – depending on your church tradition. And today we remember that first occasion when they were spoken by Jesus 'on the night he was betrayed' (1 Corinthians 11:23). We are looking back this whole week to those events, slung between Palm Sunday and Easter Day. And it is utterly right that we should do so, for our Christian faith is founded on historical events, not religious experience or speculation. Facts that happened. Good news to be proclaimed. 'It is finished!' There is an essential 'having-happened-ness' about the gospel that we must never forget, and this annual Holy Week and our regular participation in the Lord's Supper will ensure that we never do. We look back with thanks and faith.

For the Jews, of course, the dynamic is the same. Passover is when they too look back, remembering and reliving the great historic act of God's redemption, the exodus. So Jesus makes careful and probably secret arrangements to share the Passover with his disciples in a place where they could be undisturbed, having spent the previous days surrounded by people in the temple courts (21:37–38).

Our last Passover . . .

They gather around the familiar feast, with the roast lamb ('the Passover' itself) there in the midst of them. And Jesus says some unexpected words. First of all, he tells them how strongly he has wanted to share this Passover with them 'before I suffer' – by which, of course, he means his death. He has warned them of this before, but has it really sunk in? Now it should do. 'This will be our last Passover together, friends . . . in this world.'

. . . until the kingdom of God comes

He will not eat the Passover with them again, or drink the fruit of the vine (the term they used when giving thanks for the cups of wine at Passover), 'until it (meaning the Passover itself) finds fulfilment in the kingdom of God' (verses 16 and 18). Jesus is turning this meal from something that commemorates the *past* (which it must continue to do, of course) into an anticipation of the *future*. It has become something yet to be 'fulfilled'.

Jesus had announced the arrival of the kingdom of God in and through himself already. But he also clearly taught that the kingdom would grow and be fully consummated in the future. And that is what he means here. He anticipates the joy of the great feast of the Messiah, drawing on scriptures such as Isaiah 25:6, and reminding his hearers of the times he has pictured the future as a great banquet (Luke 14:15–24). *Then*, says Jesus, I shall eat and drink with you again to celebrate the fulfilment of God's great redemption – the ultimate redemption that will surpass the exodus and Passover themselves.[1]

Hebrews tells us that it was 'for the joy set before him' that Jesus 'endured the cross, scorning its shame, and sat down at the right hand of the throne of God' (Hebrews 12:2). Part of that future joy was doubtless the anticipation of eating again with sisters and brothers with whom he had shared those three years on earth – and with the millions more who would come to believe in him through their witness.

---

1 Some people think that Jesus is referring to his future presence with his disciples, after his death and resurrection, when they will share the Lord's Supper together. But there is no suggestion in the New Testament that Jesus *eats* with us in those moments. (It would be strange to think of him doing so, since the bread and wine represent his body and blood.) Also, what Jesus says here refers to the eschatological messianic banquet in the new creation (the fulfilment of Passover). It is not contradicted by the fact that Jesus did eat with his disciples in his resurrection body (Luke 24:41–43; Acts 1:4).

Today, we celebrate the Last Supper – except that it won't be the last! The best is yet to come. The wedding feast of the Lamb awaits and blessed are those who invited – which includes us all (Revelation 19:9). Holy Communion will always be a *remembrance* of the cross. But we ought to emphasize that it is also an *anticipation* of the future that the cross has accomplished for us. Let it be so for you today.

And so, Father, calling to mind his death on the cross,
his perfect sacrifice made once for all for the sins of all people,
rejoicing at his mighty resurrection and glorious ascension,
and looking for his coming in glory,
we celebrate this memorial of our redemption.
(From the liturgy of Holy Communion, *The Alternative Service Book 1980*)

Good Friday
The new and greater exodus
Bible reading: Romans 8:18–39

At last, the day Lent has been preparing us for, the day on which Christ cried out, 'It is finished' – that triumphant claim whose multiple dimensions we have been exploring.

Can there be anywhere better to go today than to this sublime passage in Romans 8? It is so rich in content, so sparkling with gospel jewels, that it is hard to know where to start. Let's do so in the climactic final section (verses 31–39), with Paul's four rhetorical questions, since his answer to each of them is essentially the same – the cross of Christ!

1 *Who can be against us?* Nobody, for God gave up his Son (to death) and will give us everything else needed for our protection.
2 *Who can bring any charge against us?* Nobody, for God has declared us righteous (through the atoning sacrifice of his Son; 3:25–26).
3 *Who condemns us?* Nobody, for the Messiah died for us – and has been raised to life as our vindicator and advocate.
4 *What can separate us from the love of Christ?* Nothing, for he loved us even unto death (5:6–8).

Rest assured, then, that what happened on that first Good Friday is your eternal guarantee. The love of God that took Jesus to the cross is the love from which nothing can separate you – ever.

Nothing in all creation
Paul triumphantly calls out a whole list of things that, no matter how powerful and threatening they seem, can never separate us

from God's love in the Messiah Jesus, our Lord. He climaxes with 'nor anything else in all creation' (verse 39). And why not? First of all, because Christ is Lord over the whole of creation, and has reconciled it to God through his blood shed on the cross, as Paul so emphatically declares in Colossians 1:15–20 (Wednesday's reading). Under the authority of the Crucified, creation itself cannot ultimately stand against us or separate us from him.

Second, nothing in creation can separate us because creation shares with us in the great liberation from bondage that Christ has accomplished – which takes us back to the first half of our passage, and especially verses 18–21. Just as the Israelites groaned in their slavery, so we and creation also groan. Just as the Israelites longed with hope for their salvation, so do we, along with creation.

The new exodus

Yesterday we saw how Christ transformed the Passover from a memorial of the exodus into an anticipation of the future consummated kingdom of God, as well as a remembrance of his own 'exodus' accomplished in Jerusalem (Luke 9:31). Today, Paul transforms the exodus narrative from a story about the children of Israel being released from bondage in Egypt into the prototype of the whole-Bible narrative of how creation and the children of God, together, will be released from bondage to frustration, decay and death, into the freedom and glory that God plans for it and for us. This is cosmic-level exodus. No wonder creation responded, as it did at the first exodus, to God's even greater redemptive act. The sun was darkened and the earth quaked on Good Friday, and the earth quaked again as God raised his Son from the dead on Easter Day.

There is no doubt here that Paul, as elsewhere in his writings, is portraying the great liberating gospel story as a greater exodus, as God's ultimate act of redemption and liberation for us and for all creation. For just as creation suffers as it shares the bondage caused by our sin, so we shall share in the glory of its liberation, and all creation will rejoice with us (as Psalm 96 celebrated). Paul thinks of us being saved not *out of* the earth, but *along with* the earth.

Good Friday is exodus-shaped and creation-wide. Let the grandeur of that vista capture your mind today.

Whatever challenges you face (even some you might recognize in verses 37–39), there is nothing in all creation – ruled and reconciled by the crucified and risen Christ – that can ultimately stand against you or separate you from God's love.

Not one thing.

Holy Saturday
The new heaven and new earth

Bible reading: Revelation 21:1–5;
21:22 – 22:5

Today is the one and only day when we remember a dead Christ. It is as if creation held its breath, pausing between the triumph of his atoning death and the vindication of his glorious resurrection. It also gives us time to pause and look back over the journey, on this last day of Lent, and remember all we have seen and learned together.

Six great viewpoints

I arranged for us to visit six great viewpoints, and I hope you have felt inspired and nourished by the vistas and horizons of biblical truth at each spot. We have explored six massive biblical themes, each profoundly connected to the cross, and each a part of what Jesus knew he had accomplished when he cried out, 'It is finished!'

Why not pause and look back at the Table of Contents, at those six headings for the weeks of Lent, and give thanks again for all that God accomplished through the cross of Christ?

The whole Bible story

But I had another intention behind the journey, which I hope you will have observed en route. At each viewpoint I directed your gaze to texts from all over Scripture – Old Testament, Gospels and Epistles. For the journey we have been on is nothing less than the journey of the great biblical story itself. That story takes us from God's good creation, so spoiled and broken by our sin, through

God's promises and object lessons of sin and salvation in Old Testament Israel, on to the central act of the story, the incarnation, life, teaching, atoning death, resurrection and ascension of Jesus the Messiah. And then the Bible story propels us forward through the mission of the church, to the final judgment and the new creation.

Not an ending, but a new beginning

And so today's reading from the Bible's awe-inspiring final two chapters challenges our imagination to 'see' with John some glimpses of the future – *not* when we all go off to heaven, but when God comes to make his dwelling among his redeemed humanity in his purged and renewed creation.

Have you noticed how many times it says, 'No more', or 'No longer'? All that will *not* be in the new creation will *not* be there because it was dealt with by Christ's victory on the cross.

There will be no more:

- *sea* (21:1). The sea represented chaotic, restless, rebellious evil in Old Testament symbolism, the place from which the rampaging beasts in Daniel's visions had come to trample the nations;
- *death, mourning, crying or pain* (21:4). All sufferings will be ended, for there will be nothing any longer to cause them;
- *sin,* for there will be no more sinners (21:7–8); the new creation involves exclusion as well as inclusion – exclusion of the unrepentantly and persistently wicked;
- *darkness and night* (21:25; 22:5), or all that they represent. The light of God's presence will dispel the darkest evils;
- *impurity, shame or deceit* (22:27) – those essential fingerprints of our fallenness – all gone;
- *international strife* (22:2), for the nations will find healing through the leaves of the tree of life and the river of life. And above all . . .
- *curse* (22:7). Lamech's longing will be granted (Genesis 5:28–29). The earth will be freed from futility and its redeemed inhabitants will be freed from bondage to its curse.

And all that *will* be there in the new creation will be there because of the victory of the cross of Christ. Hallelujah!

Read through Revelation 21 – 22 again as you prepare your heart and mind for Easter Day, and fill in this list of the features John mentions: the unalloyed covenant presence of God – Immanuel fulfilled; the beauty of the bride of the Lamb; the beauty, size and security of the city of God; the glory of human civilization (not obliterated, but) purged of all sin, redeemed and brought into God's city for God's glory; life; light; healing; peace; the joy of serving and reigning with Christ in God's new creation for ever.

And then spend time thanking God for this wonderful prospect. For this is not just the end of our journey this Lent. It is the end of the journey of the whole Bible. The end of one journey, but the beginning of the next.

EASTER DAY

Like his glorious body

Bible reading: Revelation 1:9–18

I, John, your brother and companion in the suffering and kingdom and patient endurance that are ours in Jesus, was on the island of Patmos because of the word of God and the testimony of Jesus. On the Lord's Day I was in the Spirit, and I heard behind me a loud voice like a trumpet, which said: 'Write on a scroll what you see and send it to the seven churches: to Ephesus, Smyrna, Pergamum, Thyatira, Sardis, Philadelphia and Laodicea.'

I turned around to see the voice that was speaking to me. And when I turned I saw seven golden lampstands, and among the lampstands was someone like a son of man dressed in a robe reaching down to his feet and with a golden sash around his chest. The hair on his head was white like wool, as white as snow, and his eyes were like blazing fire. His feet were like bronze glowing in a furnace, and his voice was like the sound of rushing waters. In his right hand he held seven stars, and coming out of his mouth was a sharp, double-edged sword. His face was like the sun shining in all its brilliance.

When I saw him, I fell at his feet as though dead. Then he placed his right hand on me and said: 'Do not be afraid. I am the First and the Last. I am the Living One; I was dead, and now look, I am alive for ever and ever! And I hold the keys of death and Hades.'
(Revelation 1:9–18)

The Lord Jesus Christ . . . will transform our lowly bodies so that they will be like his glorious body.
(Philippians 3:20–21)

Christ's conquest of death also indicates the nature of resurrection. Firstly, the risen Lord was not a resuscitated corpse. We do not believe that our bodies will be miraculously reconstituted out of the identical material particles of which they are at present composed. Jesus performed three resuscitations during his ministry, restoring to this life the son of the widow of Nain, Jairus's daughter and Lazarus. One understands the sympathy that C. S. Lewis expressed for Lazarus. 'To be brought back,' he wrote, 'and have all one's dying to do again was rather hard.' But Jesus's resurrection was not a resuscitation. He was raised to an altogether new plane of existence in which he was no longer mortal but 'alive for ever and ever' (Rev. 1:18).

Secondly, our Christian hope of resurrection is not merely the survival of the soul. As Jesus himself said, 'It is I myself! Touch me and see; a ghost does not have flesh and bones, as you see I have' (Luke 24:39). So the risen Lord was neither a revived corpse nor an immaterial ghost. Instead, he was raised from death and simultaneously changed into a new vehicle for his personality. Moreover, our resurrection body will be like his, and his was a remarkable combination of continuity and discontinuity. On the one hand, there was a clear link between his two bodies. The scars were still there in his hands, feet and side, and Mary Magdalene recognized his voice. On the other hand, his body passed through the grave clothes, out of the sealed tomb, and through locked doors. So it evidently had new and undreamed-of powers.

The apostle Paul illustrated this combination from the relation between seeds and flowers. The continuity ensures that each seed produces its own flower. But the discontinuity is more striking, since out of a plain and even ugly little seed will spring a fragrant, colorful and elegant flower. 'So will it be with the resurrection of the dead' (1 Cor. 15:42). To sum up, what we are looking forward to is neither a resuscitation (in which we are raised but not changed) nor a survival (in which we are changed into a ghost but not raised bodily) but a resurrection (in which we are both raised and changed, transfigured and glorified simultaneously).

John Stott, *Through the Bible through the Year*, p. 284

Resurrected. Raised, changed, transfigured and glorified for ever, all because of our Radical Reconciler.

Hallelujah!

References

By John Stott

The Cross of Christ (Nottingham: IVP, 2006)
The Incomparable Christ (Nottingham: IVP, 2014)
Through the Bible through the Year (Oxford: Lion Hudson, 2014)

Other references

The Alternative Service Book 1980 (Cambridge, Colchester and London: Cambridge University Press, William Clowes Ltd and SPCK, 1980)

Bock, Darrell L., *Luke: The IVP New Testament Commentary Series* (Downers Grove, Ill.: InterVarsity Press, 1994)

Caird, George B., *A Commentary on the Revelation of St John the Divine* (London: A&C Black, 1966)

The Cape Town Commitment: A Confession of Faith and a Call to Action (The Lausanne Movement, 2011; <www.lausanne.org>)

Duckworth, Marilyn, *Disorderly Conduct* (Auckland: Hodder & Stoughton, 1984)

Marshall, I. Howard, *1 Peter* (Downers Grove, Ill.: InterVarsity Press, 1991)

Meynell, Mark, *When Darkness Seems My Closest Friend: Reflections on Life and Ministry with Depression* (London: IVP, 2018)

Wright, Christopher J. H., *The God I Don't Understand: Reflections on Tough Questions of Faith* (Grand Rapids, Mich.: Zondervan, 2008)

Wright, Tom, *Paul for Everyone: The Prison Letters – Ephesians, Philippians, Colossians and Philemon* (London: SPCK, 2002)